PETER

by Stacy Sobieski

samuelfrench.co.uk

ISBN 978-0-573-11368-0

www.samuelfrench.co.uk

www.samuelfrench.com

FOR AMATEUR PRODUCTION ENQUIRIES

UNITED KINGDOM AND WORLD EXCLUDING NORTH AMERICA
plays@SamuelFrench-London.co.uk
020 7255 4302/01

UNITED STATES AND CANADA
info@SamuelFrench.com
1-866-598-8449

Each title is subject to availability from Samuel French, depending upon country of performance.

THINKING ABOUT PERFORMING A SHOW?

There are thousands of plays and musicals available to perform from Samuel French right now, and applying for a licence is easier and more affordable than you might think

From classic plays to brand new musicals, from monologues to epic dramas, there are shows for everyone.

Plays and musicals are protected by copyright law so if you want to perform them, the first thing you'll need is a licence. This simple process helps support the playwright by ensuring they get paid for their work, and means that you'll have the documents you need to stage the show in public.

Not all our shows are available to perform all the time, so it's important to check and apply for a licence before you start rehearsals or commit to doing the show.

LEARN MORE & FIND THOUSANDS OF SHOWS

Browse our full range of plays and musicals and find out more about how to license a show

www.samuelfrench.co.uk/perform

Talk to the friendly experts in our Licensing team for advice on choosing a show, and help with licensing

plays@samuelfrench.co.uk   020 7387 9373

Acting Editions

BORN TO PERFORM

Playscripts designed from the ground up to work the way you do in rehearsal, performance and study

---

Larger, clearer text for easier reading

Wider margins for notes

Performance features such as character and props lists, sound and lighting cues, and more

---

+ CHOOSE A SIZE AND STYLE TO SUIT YOU

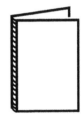

STANDARD EDITION

Our regular paperback book at our regular size

SPIRAL-BOUND EDITION

The same size as the Standard Edition, but with a sturdy, easy-to-fold, easy-to-hold spiral-bound spine

LARGE EDITION

A4 size and spiral bound, with larger text and a blank page for notes opposite every page of text. Perfect for technical and directing use

---

LEARN MORE **samuelfrench.co.uk/actingeditions**

AUTHOR'S NOTE

As a theatergoer, I've always been fond of the Kneehigh/Shared Experience type of theatrical approach. Rather than employing intricate sets and an army of stagehands, the audience is simply asked to use their imaginations. With this kind of approach, the possibility for play is endless. A ladder can suddenly become a lavish sailboat, a singular strobe light can give us the impression of an oncoming train, and (by throwing realism out the window) two people can literally swing from the chandeliers in a deliciously heightened expression of their euphoria. And all the while, the audience happily accepts this as being so. It's one of the perks of working in such a magical art form.

As such, *PETER* need not possess a great sense of "realism". The set itself could be quite minimalistic (thus allowing for the transitions between scenes to be as easy and seamless as possible) and bold creative choices can certainly be utilized throughout the play, especially in the final scene. The scene changes themselves need not be masked, but could become rather like a kind of dance between the past and the present.

In short, there should be a sense of magic and play to the piece.

ABOUT THE AUTHOR

Stacy Sobieski is an American writer and actress. She currently resides in London.

Special Thanks

Michael and Micki Sobieski, the Birmingham School of Acting (namely Lise Olson and the late David Vann), Sell A Door Theatre Company, David Hutchinson, Phillip Rowntree, Amy Burke, the Great Ormond Street Hospital, Suzan and Randy Buchmiller, Alastair Ballantyne, the Jorgensen family, Andrew Birkin, and everyone at Samuel French Ltd.

Peter was first performed as a staged reading at the
Birmingham School of Acting on 10 June, 2011.
It was directed by Lise Olson and featured the following cast:

PETER   **Robert Durbin**
J.M. BARRIE   **Alan Magor**
SYLVIA   **Emma Boyle**
GEORGE   **Sam Thompson**
JACK   **Jacob Kohli**
MARY HODGSON   **Joy McDermott**
ARTHUR   **Philip Jennings**
MARY ANSELL   **Evelyn Campbell**
PEGGY   **Amalia Vitale**

Peter received its world premiere at the LOST Theatre in London
on
23 October, 2012, produced by Sell A Door Theatre Company.
It was directed by David Hutchinson and featured the following
cast:

PETER   **Martin Richardson**
J.M. BARRIE   **Stewart Marquis**
SYLVIA   **Jemma Hines**
GEORGE   **Mark Fountain**
PEGGY/ JACK   **Evelyn Campbell**
MARY HODGSON   **Helen Fullerton**
ARTHUR   **Tom Gordon-Gill**
MARY ANSELL   **Stacy Sobieski**

This play is dedicated to the mysterious stranger I met all those years ago by the Peter Pan statue in Kensington Gardens, who encouraged me to write.

BARRIE Well, it's not a very respectable career, is it? Interesting perhaps, at times, but not what one would call a proper vocation. Would I had chosen a better career for myself.

SYLVIA And what would you have considered to be a better choice?

BARRIE Well, my mother had high hopes that I would become a respectable minister. I believe that would have been quite a satisfactory vocation. But I could never come to terms with the image I had of all five foot three-and-a-half inches of me preaching the word of God while all the while struggling in vain to see over the pulpit.

SYLVIA *(tickled by this)* Five foot three and a *half*?

BARRIE Yes, that half-inch is very important to me.

SYLVIA Of course. And so instead you chose to be a writer?

BARRIE Or rather, it chose me. Some men must write, Mrs. Davies. They can do nothing else.

SYLVIA Then tell me, how do you choose the subject on which you write about?

BARRIE I write about whatever intrigues me. Desert islands, shipwrecks. Happiest is he who writes of adventure.[3]

SYLVIA My boys adore a good adventure tale. They're always playing at pirates and indians. Many a time have I had to rescue their poor nursemaid after they've taken her prisoner and tied her to a tree.

BARRIE Tell me, how old are your sons?

SYLVIA George is eleven, Jack is ten, and Peter is just a babe.

BARRIE Ah, all under twelve. How splendid. Nothing that happens after we are twelve matters very much.[4] If you ask me, the end of boyhood is the end of a life worth living.[5]

SYLVIA Do you really believe that, Mr. Barrie?

BARRIE Oh absolutely. Do you know, the horror of my boyhood was that I knew a time would come when I must give up the games, and how it was to be done, I saw not.[6] I didn't want to give up my marbles and become a man. So there was only one solution as far as I was concerned *(leaning in)*: I knew I must continue playing in secret... Do you know what genius is, Mrs. Davies? It is the power to be a boy again at will.[7]

SYLVIA That is indeed a wonderful thing, but surely the end of boyhood isn't the end of a life worth living. Why, think of all the adventures that are still ahead of them: university, marriage, children, a career.

BARRIE Yes, but in boyhood, you are blissfully unaware. The world is a magical place where nothing can touch you or bring you down. With adulthood comes sorrow and loss. There comes a melancholy awareness which never existed before. And how can you truly enjoy those things that you speak of, children and marriage and a career, when you know that the end is always lurking ahead?

SYLVIA You speak of death, Mr. Barrie?

BARRIE Yes, I suppose I do.

SYLVIA But, Mr. Barrie, to die will be an awfully big adventure,[8] don't you think?

He looks at her with delighted awe. She has won the debate.

BARRIE Splendid. Just splendid.

Lights fade.

1.3.

A few months prior to the previous scene. Lights up on the **DAVIES***'s parlour room, where* **SYLVIA** *sits mending a pair of britches. She is a wonder with a needle and thread. Her husband,* **ARTHUR,** *is sitting nearby reading a newspaper. He's a very handsome, kind man who loves his family above all else. At length, we hear a door open and a flurry of excitement coming from the hall. Two young boys,* **GEORGE** *and* **JACK,** *come rushing in. They are both dressed in blue blouses with red velvet tam-o'-shanters. They are followed by their nursemaid,* **MARY HODGSON,** *who is carrying a young infant in her arms.*

GEORGE Mother! We have just met the most extraordinary man in Kensington Gardens!

SYLVIA Have you now?

JACK He's magic, mother! He can make his ears wiggle and his eyebrows dance —

GEORGE *(to* **ARTHUR***)* And he has a tame bear! He wrestles with it and then makes it dance with him. He's a wondrous man, Father!

ARTHUR My, I do not doubt it.

MARY *(handing the baby to* **SYLVIA***)* It was quite the exciting day, Mr. Davies. Though I can't say I myself was very impressed with the man. For one, his tame bear looked rather suspiciously like a dog to me.

GEORGE Oh Mary, stop being such a ninny.

JACK *(to* **GEORGE***)* Do you think he'll be in the gardens again tomorrow?

GEORGE I'm sure of it! Oh Mother, can we go back tomorrow? If we don't go he is sure to forget all about us.

SYLVIA I don't see why you shouldn't.

GEORGE And you must come with us, Father! And you too, Mother!

SYLVIA Well I don't know about that, my dear. Your father has to be at the office tomorrow, and we shall both be out awfully late tonight.

GEORGE Where are you going?

SYLVIA Your father and I have a dinner party to attend this evening.

The boys let out simultaneous groans.

GEORGE Oh Mother, *must* you go to the party tonight?

ARTHUR I'm afraid so, George. It's all part of being an adult. Sometimes you must do things even when you'd rather not.

GEORGE Well then...perhaps you could bring us back some sweets?

ARTHUR I don't think that would be very wise, my boy. You're going to rot your teeth with the amount of sweets you've been eating lately.

GEORGE But Father, it's not for me! I was thinking only of Peter *(gesturing to the baby in SYLVIA's arms)*. I think he would be ever so grateful if you brought him back some sweets from the party.

SYLVIA *smiles at this.*

ARTHUR Well, perhaps when Peter is old enough to ask for such things himself, then we shall bring him some. But until that time, there will be no more sweets in this house.

As ARTHUR returns to his paper, GEORGE lets out a defeated sigh. He looks dejectedly at SYLVIA, who then smiles and shoots him a sly wink. GEORGE's face lights up. SYLVIA then puts a finger to her lips, swearing him to secrecy. He nods knowingly.

JACK Will you read to us before you go to the party, Mother?

SYLVIA Of course, darling. But I must first finish mending your britches. Soon you will have torn every pair you own and then

I shall have to send you to the park in your baptism frock, for it will be the only bit of clothing you have left.

GEORGE Oh no, Mother! I shall go naked to the park if I have to. I daresay I would rather prefer it.

MARY Come now, George. Upstairs and into the bath with you.

GEORGE *starts to make a run for it but* MARY, *already anticipating his attempted escape, catches him and scoops him up under her arm.*

GEORGE *(defiantly, as he is carried out)* I won't be bathed, Mary! I tell you I will not be bathed!

MARY *(as she goes)* You too, Jack!

JACK *obediently goes to follow, then stops for a moment and turns back to* SYLVIA.

JACK Mother, how did we get to know you?[9]

SYLVIA Why, I have known you since before you were even born.

JACK *(after some contemplation)* What hour was I born?[10]

SYLVIA At precisely half past two in the morning.

JACK Oh, Mother, I hope I didn't wake you!

SYLVIA *(tickled by this)* It was perfectly all right, my dear. Your father and I couldn't wait to meet you.

JACK, *satisfied with this response, turns to go. Just before he exits, he turns back to* SYLVIA *one last time.*

JACK Mother?

SYLVIA Yes, darling?

JACK Mother, I am glad of you.[11]

With this, he goes skipping from the room. ARTHUR *and* SYLVIA *smile at each other.* ARTHUR *rises and kisses* SYLVIA *on the forehead. A loud crash is heard upstairs, followed by victorious boyish laughter and a cry of aggravation from* MARY.

ARTHUR I'd better go help Mary.

ARTHUR *starts for the stairs.*

(Playfully yelling up the stairs as he goes) A little less noise there! A little less noise![12]

SYLVIA *smiles and looks lovingly at the infant in her arms.*

SYLVIA And what did you think of this man, Peter?

Lights fade.

1.4.

Fast-forward to summer, 1921. A handsome **PETER LLEWELYN DAVIES** *in his early twenties sits on a bench in Kensington Gardens. He appears to be waiting somewhat anxiously for someone. Projected onto the back wall of the stage is an image of the famous Peter Pan statue, commissioned by* **J.M. BARRIE** *in 1912. The statue will serve as a kind of constant observer during all of* **PETER** *and* **MARY**'s *future meetings. At length,* **PETER** *sees someone approaching and leaps to his feet. It's his old nursemaid,* **MARY HODGSON.**

MARY Oh my sweet Peter!

PETER *embraces her, lifting her off the ground.*

PETER Hello Mary, old girl! I'm glad you could come!

MARY *(playfully hitting him)* Oh Peter, put me down! *(***PETER** *sets her down)* Well now, when did you get to be taller than me? It used to be me who would lift *you.*

PETER *(almost bashfully)* It's been quite a while since those days. I'm grown up now.

MARY *smiles. They sit.*

Have you been well?

MARY Yes, I have. I lead a much quieter life now that you boys are grown.

PETER A welcome change, no doubt.

MARY I suppose, in a way. But I wouldn't have traded those days for anything.

PETER To be honest, I was a bit hesitant about getting in touch. It's been quite some time since we last spoke. Though of course I can understand your silence.

MARY Well, when your ward takes up with a woman twice his age, it comes as quite a shock.

PETER Yes, of course.

MARY And to not come home while you were on leave because you preferred to stay holed up with *her*, well, I won't pretend that I wasn't upset.

PETER I have no excuse except to say that I thought I was in love. And love will make even the best of men behave irrationally.

MARY With a woman nearly the same age as your mother?

PETER I know it seems odd, Mary. But age just wasn't an issue with us. Vera had more energy and vitality about her than any girl I ever met while at school.

MARY And her husband? Was he an "issue"?

PETER (*softly yet resolutely*) I can't say that I'm proud of what I've done, but I will say that I don't regret a minute of it.

MARY *sees that continuing the argument would be futile. She sighs in defeat.*

MARY Would you believe that our disapproval of the whole thing was the one time Barrie and I have ever seen eye to eye about something? So I suppose, really, I should thank you.

PETER For what?

MARY For inciting a miracle.

PETER *laughs at this.*

PETER How is he, Mary?

MARY The little genius? We try to keep our distance as much as possible, but the last I saw Mr. Barrie, he was well.

PETER You mean to tell me that you *still* don't get along?

MARY (*smiling*) Yes, well, some things never change.

PETER You always were quite the stubborn one.

MARY Yes, but never without cause. I have always had my reasons.

PETER And what exactly were your "reasons" for disliking him?

MARY *considers her response for a moment.*

MARY Your mother and I just had different opinions of the man, that's all.

PETER Mary, I'm not a child anymore. You can speak freely with me.

Another moment of hesitation from MARY.

MARY It wasn't necessarily anything that he said or did. I just... didn't see the point of it all, really. You already had a father, a mother *and* me, what did you need him for? But now that I say it out loud, it sounds like such a petty reason to dislike someone.

PETER Not at all.

MARY Well, regardless of my personal feelings for the man, your darling mother adored him, as did your brothers. And so I, in turn, was forced to bite my tongue.

PETER *(teasingly)* A difficult task for you, I imagine.

MARY Yes, quite. You can just imagine my agony when, as a kind of initiation into the family, you boys took to calling the intruder "Uncle Jim".

As the lights transform into the next scene, the Peter Pan statue flickers briefly and then disappears.

1.5.

1898. The same bench in Kensington Gardens, though this time the Peter Pan statue is nowhere to be found. **GEORGE** *is perched next to* **BARRIE** *on the bench while* **MARY**, *out of earshot, fusses about with* **PETER**'s *pram.*

GEORGE Uncle Jim, why is Mary such a ninny?

BARRIE I'm afraid you'll have to be more specific, my boy.

GEORGE Why does she always refuse to play with me? Instead she just stands by Peter's pram all day long like a ninny.

BARRIE Well, she's Peter's nursemaid just as much as she is yours. Besides, what if she were to turn her back to go play with you and then Peter fell out of his pram? How would you feel then?

GEORGE Peter isn't daft enough to fall out of his pram.

BARRIE You don't think he'd want to make a run for it as soon as Mary turned her back?

GEORGE What do you mean?

BARRIE All babies have the desire to dash away the second their nursemaids aren't looking. Why I once knew of a boy who, the second his nursemaid turned her back, went flying right up into the treetops as fast as he could. He was one of the few babies in history to have made a successful escape.

GEORGE You mean for me to believe that he *flew* away?

BARRIE Well of course he flew! Do you think he walked away? Ha, what a silly thought.

GEORGE *(defiantly)* Uncle Jim, babies can't fly.

BARRIE Well now, that just shows how much you have forgotten your own past. Tell me, do you ever feel a strong itch between your shoulders?[13]

GEORGE *(unsure but with total confidence)* Yes, of course.

BARRIE That's because that's where your wings used to be. You see, before you were a human, you were a bird, and some of those birdlike qualities remain with us while we're babies. That's why babies can fly, though they'd never let you see them do it.

GEORGE *looks at him sceptically.*

Alright then, do me a favour and press your fingers to your temples.

GEORGE *does so, very reluctantly.*

Now try to remember a time when you yourself wanted to fly away to the treetops.

GEORGE I don't remember a thing!

BARRIE Think harder.

GEORGE *squeezes his eyes tightly shut.*

GEORGE Still nothing.

BARRIE Come on, old boy, think harder...

For several seconds there is a moment of intense concentration. GEORGE *squeezes his temples so hard that it looks as though he might burst into a million pieces at any moment. Then, suddenly:*

GEORGE Wait... Yes, I think I remember now! I remember! I wanted to fly right up into the treetops!

BARRIE Splendid!

GEORGE How wonderful to remember a long forgotten bit of one's own past! But... Uncle Jim, why can't I fly anymore?

BARRIE Because you've lost faith in your ability to fly.

GEORGE *(sadly)* Oh.

BARRIE Nothing to feel downhearted about, my boy, we all lose our faith eventually. That's why you see all these humdrum people walking along the paths rather than playing tag in the treetops. They've all lost faith and forgotten their days as carefree birds. You see, George, the only reason birds can fly and we cannot is simply because birds have perfect faith. And to have faith is to have wings.[14]

GEORGE Then I shall go home tonight and practise leaping from my bed until I am able to fly again... Uncle Jim, what was the boy's name? The one who escaped?

MARY, *who has wandered over to them and has been listening to* **BARRIE**'*s story, rolls her eyes.*

BARRIE *(glancing over at the pram)* His name was Peter.

MARY *(interjecting)* I tell you, Mr. Barrie, I don't see any point in your telling him stories that have no moral to them.

BARRIE Don't you worry, my dear Mary. This story shall be as pure as the driven snow.

GEORGE Was Peter's surname the same as mine?

BARRIE Lord no. What a coincidence that would be! *(Thinking on his toes)* His name was Pan. Peter Pan. And when he made his daring escape, do you know where he flew?

GEORGE Where?

BARRIE Right here to Kensington Gardens. In fact *(pointing to the spot where the Peter Pan statue will later stand)*, he landed in that spot right over there.

GEORGE Why did he come here?

BARRIE Because this park is magical. Did you know that at night, after lockout time, hundreds of mischievous fairies come out of their hiding places and sing and dance on the flowers?

GEORGE Really?

BARRIE Certainly. And did you also know that in that river right over there lies a drowned forest? Sometimes if you peer over the water's edge, you can just make it out.

MARY, *intrigued, has begun to draw closer to them in order to better hear the story.*

You see, George, by day this might seem like an ordinary park. But it's only pretending in order to protect its secret. The truth is that it's a magical, mysterious place. And if you're open to it, you'll begin to notice extraordinary things happening right under your nose. Why, if you keep your eyes peeled, you might even see a fairy skipping about.

GEORGE I should like that!

BARRIE So you see, *that* is why Peter Pan chose to come here.

GEORGE Uncle Jim, what does Pan mean?

BARRIE *(glancing at* **MARY***)* Well, perhaps Mary could tell us?

MARY No, I don't believe I know.

BARRIE Ah, no matter. You see, Pan, my dear boy... *(He pauses a moment for effect as* **GEORGE** *and* **MARY** *lean in)* ...is the Greek God who symbolised paganism and the amoral world.

MARY's face quickly changes from extreme interest into a scowl.

GEORGE Uncle Jim, what's paganism?

MARY Never mind that, George.

GEORGE But Mary, I want to know!

MARY *(looking disapprovingly at* **BARRIE***)* As pure as the driven snow, Mr. Barrie?

BARRIE Oh yes... I suppose that slipped my mind for a moment. My sincerest apologies, dear Mary.

Summoning all of her willpower, **MARY** *bites her tongue, does an about-face and storms off.*

GEORGE *(delighted)* Splendid!

Lights fade.

1.6.

As the previous scene fades into the shadows, the Peter Pan statue flickers back into existence and the lights rise on **MARY** *and twenty-year old* **PETER**, *still seated on the bench. A reflective quiet has descended over them.*

PETER How did the news reach you?

MARY I was upstairs in my room when I heard knocking at the front door. Barrie was already downstairs so he was the first to reach the entryway. When I got to the landing I heard him let out a wail fit for a banshee. That said it all. I knew in that moment, George was dead.

For a moment they sit in silence.

How did it happen?

PETER What do you mean?

MARY They never told me the specifics of it all. Back then women weren't to know such grisly details if it could be helped.

PETER Mary, I don't think —

MARY Please, Peter. I'd like to know.

For a moment **PETER** *considers not telling her. Then...*

PETER It's no grand story, really. His battalion was in Flanders at the time, and he was sitting on a bank with the other soldiers. Then suddenly he just went limp. He had been shot through the head.

Beat.

They say he died almost instantly, so perhaps he didn't feel much pain.

MARY What a horrid business.

PETER To be honest, when I first went into the trenches, I daresay I was looking forward to taking part in a fight. But now that I've experienced the true horror of it, I shall never again have any such desire.

MARY Was it as terrible as the papers say?

PETER Yes. Modern artillery fire is damnable beyond all powers of description. You crouch down in the bottom of your trench and listen helplessly to the whispering noise which comes before the crash of each heavy shell. Each near one seems to be coming straight at you. It's rather like that dream one has of falling through space, and waking up before one reaches the bottom, only instead of waiting for the bottom, one waits for the burst of the shell.[15] And to then see the hundreds of bodies lying motionless on the field, their skin that horrible colour of dirty chalk... Well, it's all just too terrible.

MARY Do you think you'll be able to put it behind you, now that you're home?

PETER *(after some thought)* Yes, perhaps... *(Then, simply)* Still, I don't feel as friendly towards the moon as I once did.[16]

Lights fade.

1.7.

SYLVIA *and* BARRIE'*s wife*, MARY *(known in her stage career as* MARY ANSELL*), are sat around a garden table drinking tea.* MARY *is a lovely, graceful creature. The sounds of* BARRIE *and the boys playing and laughing can be heard in the distance.*

MARY ANSELL It's very kind of you to have us over, Mrs. Davies.

SYLVIA Please, call me Sylvia.

MARY ANSELL Well then, you must call me Mary. What a lovely home this is.

SYLVIA That's very kind of you to say. Though I apologise that it isn't the most peaceful of atmospheres, what with three boys running around.

ARTHUR *enters with an impressive assortment of biscuits. He places it on the table and sits in one of the vacant chairs.*

MARY ANSELL I daresay my husband is partially to blame for that. He has a gift for bringing out the rowdy tendencies of young boys.

ARTHUR Three boys can be quite a handful, but we wouldn't trade them for the world.

MARY ANSELL Are you planning on having any more?

SYLVIA *and* ARTHUR *exchange a glance.*

I'm terribly sorry, it's not my place to ask.

SYLVIA Not at all. Actually, it seems that we already have another one on the way. A boy, we think. I know one can't really know these things for certain, but my gut feeling is that it's another boy.

MARY ANSELL How wonderful for you!

A scream is heard offstage. It's **MARY HODGSON**. *The boys holler victoriously.*

ARTHUR We haven't had the heart to tell poor Mary yet.

MARY ANSELL Have you chosen a name?

SYLVIA We were thinking of calling him Michael.

MARY ANSELL How splendid. Three boys and another one on the way. How I would adore that.

ARTHUR We consider ourselves very fortunate.

SYLVIA I'm sure it won't be long until you and Jimmy have little ones of your own. Though it must be nice to be able to focus your energies on your career?

MARY ANSELL To be honest, I've not done much acting since I married.

ARTHUR Do you think you'll ever take it up again?

MARY ANSELL Yes, perhaps I will one day. After all, it wouldn't be hard to come by a good role. Having a famous playwright for a husband does have its advantages. Though to be honest with you, I would give it all up entirely for the chance to become a mother.

SYLVIA Well, if the way Jimmy is with our boys is any indication, I'm sure that day isn't very far off. He's so wonderful with children, I'm sure he's dying to start a family of his own.

MARY ANSELL Oh, yes, of course.

At this, **MARY HODGSON** *enters. She appears frazzled and agitated.*

MARY I tell you, Mrs. Davies, there's no talking to them when they're like this. I tried get them to take their medicine and they nearly shot my arm off with one of their bow and arrows.

SYLVIA Oh, dear Mary. I'm so sorry.

ARTHUR Perhaps I should have a go at it?

MARY If you feel up to the challenge, be my guest.

MARY hands the medicine bottle to **ARTHUR**.

(As **ARTHUR** *exits)* God speed to you, Mr. Davies.

SYLVIA Won't you sit down and have some tea with us, Mary?

MARY Oh, yes, thank you. A bit of tea to calm my nerves would be lovely.

MARY *sits as* **SYLVIA** *pours her a cup of tea.*

I simply don't know what to do anymore, Mrs. Davies. They're completely out of control. And I daresay Mr. Barrie is the worst of them all. *(Realising that she's in* **MARY**'s *presence)* Oh I beg your pardon, Mrs. Barrie. I only meant that —

MARY ANSELL It's quite all right. In fact, I couldn't agree with you more.

SYLVIA What have they gotten up to now, Mary?

MARY They've strapped a tiger mask on that poor dog of Mr. Barrie's and have taken him prisoner. They've also stolen my hat and hung it from a tree branch. I can only assume they're using it as bait, but I won't be falling for that one twice.

Suddenly, **BARRIE** *enters. He is dressed like a ragtag pirate and is wheezing and coughing.*

MARY ANSELL *(embarrassed)* Mr. Barrie, what on earth are you doing?

BARRIE Never mind me, Mrs. Barrie. I've just come out of the fray for a moment to catch my breath.

MARY *(haughtily)* Well, I suppose I shall take this opportunity to recapture my hat. I'll be back for my tea in a moment, Mrs. Davies.

She exits.

BARRIE I say, this was all much easier when I was younger.

SYLVIA Would you care for a cup of tea?

BARRIE No, thank you. Jack has just taken the prisoner to camp and I must get back before the interrogation begins.

MARY ANSELL But Mr. Barrie, the Davies were kind enough to invite us over for tea, the least you could do is oblige them with a few moments of your time. They've just told me the most wonderful news —

BARRIE Oh, Sylvia and Arthur don't mind. They can tell me their news once we've finished with our game. Sylvia, am I quite alright to carry on with the boys?

SYLVIA Oh, well... Yes, I suppose so.

BARRIE Splendid! You see, Mrs. Barrie? Quite alright. Back into the fray I go!

With that, he is gone. MARY *tries to hide her embarrassment.*

MARY ANSELL I do apologise.

SYLVIA It's quite alright. Our boys are no doubt more entertaining than us anyway.

At this, ARTHUR *re-enters.*

How did it go, dear?

ARTHUR A raging success. Though I think poor Mary has little hope of recapturing her hat any time soon. They've got the entire place rigged.

SYLVIA Oh Mary, Jimmy mentioned that you're planning to purchase a cottage at Black Lake. What a lovely place for a holiday home. You must tell us all about it.

ARTHUR Is that so? Perhaps we could bring the boys for a visit one weekend?

SYLVIA Oh they would adore that!

MARY ANSELL *(taken aback)* I'm afraid this is the first I've heard of it.

SYLVIA Oh... But surely Jimmy has mentioned it to you. Why, he's been talking about it for weeks.

ARTHUR Perhaps he intended it to be a surprise, dear.

SYLVIA Oh no, such a thoughtful thing to do and now here I've gone and ruined a perfectly good surprise! How foolish of me! Please forgive me, Mary.

MARY ANSELL I'm sure it just slipped his mind. You know how forgetful he can be sometimes.

SYLVIA Yes, of course. But you won't say anything, will you? He'd be so upset if he knew I'd ruined your surprise.

MARY ANSELL No, of course not. You have my word.

There is a lull as no one quite knows how to proceed with the conversation.

Will you excuse me for a moment, please? I think all of the sunshine today is making me feel a bit faint.

SYLVIA Yes, of course.

MARY ANSELL Thank you ever so much. I won't be long.

MARY *leaves.* **SYLVIA** *and* **ARTHUR** *exchange glances.*

ARTHUR He hasn't told her?

SYLVIA *(gently)* Hush, Arthur. It's none of our business.

ARTHUR *smiles warmly and then gently places his hand on* **SYLVIA**'s *cheek. She smiles at him and leans in for a tender kiss. Suddenly, another scream from* **MARY HODGSON** *is heard offstage. The boys holler victoriously.*

BARRIE *(offstage)* Well done, my boys!

Lights fade.

1.8.

The following morning. Lights up on **BARRIE***'s study.* **BARRIE** *is sitting at his desk, obviously experiencing a crippling case of writer's block as he puffs on his pipe and stares blankly at the paper in front of him. He begins to write something, but then thinks better of it and crumples the paper in disgust. He then returns to his previous activity of staring blankly. Frustrated, he checks his pocket watch for the time. As he does this, a bright, twinkling glimmer from the watch is reflected on the wall. This catches his eye. He begins to toy with the watch, turning it from side to side and watching as the light bounces around the room as if it were a living being. He giggles with childish delight.*

BARRIE Why hello there, little pixie.

As he chuckles and plays, **MARY ANSELL** *appears in the doorway. She observes* **BARRIE** *for a few moments before speaking.*

MARY ANSELL *(warmly)* I thought perhaps you'd like to take a walk with me. It's such a lovely day outside.

BARRIE *(as he puts the watch away)* I'm afraid I'm very busy, my dear.

MARY ANSELL Yes, I see that... Well perhaps you'd like to get tea with me this afternoon?

BARRIE *(with little emotion)* I'm dreadfully sorry, my dear, but I've already promised George that I would take him to the Savoy this afternoon for high tea.

MARY ANSELL Perhaps I could join you?

BARRIE Oh no, George would never have that. He so despises the female gender, as all boys of his age do. Don't take it personally, dear.

MARY ANSELL No. Of course not... Did Sylvia tell you her news?

BARRIE No, I suppose it slipped her mind.

MARY ANSELL They're expecting another child.

BARRIE *(looking up)* Oh?

MARY ANSELL Another boy, they think. They plan to call him Michael.

BARRIE Well, how splendid for them. I shall write them a letter of congratulations at once.

MARY ANSELL A household full of boys. It must be wonderful. Wouldn't you like it if our home were like that too? Full of children and laughter? Oh, just think of it, James —

BARRIE *(in a dismissing tone)* Please dear, I must get back to my work.

MARY ANSELL Oh. Yes, of course.

> **MARY** *turns to go but then thinks better of it. She turns back and speaks, not with particular courage but not meekly either.*

Have you given me up?[17]

BARRIE What on earth are you talking about?

MARY ANSELL Do you still love me, James?

BARRIE What a silly thing to ask.

MARY ANSELL Yes, it may be silly, but I'm asking it all the same. Do you love me?

BARRIE You are my wife.

MARY ANSELL That's not an answer, James.

BARRIE Well it's *my* answer. You are my wife and that's that.

MARY ANSELL Yes, I am your wife. But in legal terms only.

BARRIE Please, Mary, not that.

MARY ANSELL Do I disgust you?

BARRIE What an absurd thing to ask. Of course not.

MARY ANSELL   Then what is it that keeps you so far from me at night?

BARRIE   I don't know what you're talking about.

MARY ANSELL   Yes, James, you know very well what I'm talking about. You won't even let me near you.

BARRIE   I'm sorry you feel that way. Though you knew when you married me that I was a very private person.

MARY ANSELL   But I am your *wife*, James.

        BARRIE *says nothing.*

MARY ANSELL   Tell me, did you marry me for love, or was it only pity?

BARRIE   *(almost inaudibly)* Love.

MARY ANSELL   Liar.

BARRIE   Please —

MARY ANSELL   Where are our children? I want children of my own. These Davies children, they're not yours. They're not ours.

BARRIE   They love me as a father.

MARY ANSELL   They already have a father, James.

BARRIE   Please, Mary, I must get back to my work.

MARY ANSELL   I wish I knew your mind. Oh you're clever, James. I only ever loved clever men. And clever men, it seems to me, are made up of reserves. It is out of their reserves they bring their clever things. And you think they will one day open their reserves, and that you will be the favored one who is admitted to the cupboards where they keep their cleverness. But that is an illusion.[18] The only people you open your reserves to are those Davies children. You charm them with your fairy stories and they call you uncle and you think you've found something real… But one day they will grow up and forget all about you.

        MARY *exits.* **BARRIE** *sits perfectly still for several moments, staring at the blank pieces of paper lying in front of him. Then, suddenly, he is struck with an idea. He touches his pen to the paper and begins scribbling furiously. After* *a moment, he stands and begins pacing about the room, his mind overflowing with grand ideas. He then takes his place at the desk again and stares at the paper in front of him. As he does so, he lets out a laugh, almost in disbelief.*

BARRIE *(nearly in a whisper)* It will be the greatest thing they've ever read.

Lights fade.

End of Act One

ACT TWO

2.1.

SYLVIA *and* ARTHUR'*s bedroom.* ARTHUR *is perched on the edge of the bed as* SYLVIA *scurries about the room, removing clothes from the wardrobe and various dresser drawers and placing them in a suitcase.*

SYLVIA Oh darling, you're sure you don't mind?

ARTHUR Not at all, my dear. You deserve a break. I daresay a little time away will do you well.

SYLVIA It'll only be for a few days. Jimmy says he just needs to get away for a bit to clear his head. He's hoping Paris will be a good place for him to focus on this new play of his.

ARTHUR What did you say it was about again?

SYLVIA His new play? Fairies, apparently.

ARTHUR How odd. That sounds miles away from his usual subject matter. I wonder what compelled him to start writing a play about fairies...

SYLVIA It sounds like quite the ambitious project. Just yesterday he was going on and on about the latest flying contraptions. Lord only knows what he has in that head of his.

ARTHUR And are we quite sure he hasn't gone mad?

SYLVIA Oh Arthur, I daresay poor Jimmy has been mad as a hatter for quite some time. But then, I suppose that's what draws us to him.

ARTHUR And what does he plan to call this elaborate fairy play of his?

SYLVIA Originally it was to be called *The Boy Who Hated Mothers*, but our George disapproved of such a wordy title. After much debate, they finally settled on calling it *Peter Pan*.

ARTHUR Yes, well, all the best to him, I suppose. And are you to be his muse then?

SYLVIA Hardly, my darling. I suppose my job is simply to make sure that he eats and takes a moment out of his writing to enjoy the sights.

ARTHUR And Mrs. Barrie doesn't mind?

SYLVIA Apparently it was her idea.

ARTHUR How very odd... Well, I hope you know the boys and I shall miss you terribly.

SYLVIA *stops packing and perches herself on* **ARTHUR**'s *lap. She wraps her arms around his neck and kisses him lovingly on the forehead.*

SYLVIA Oh, my darling, I shall be back before you know it.

ARTHUR If only it were me sweeping you off to Paris for a lavish holiday.

SYLVIA Oh, my sweet Arthur, I don't need expensive jewellery and lavish holidays to Paris. I only need you.

She gives **ARTHUR** *a firm peck on the cheek which causes him to wince a bit.*

What is it?

ARTHUR Oh, just a bit of a pain in my cheek. Nothing to fret about.

SYLVIA A toothache? I wonder what's caused that. Let me take a look.

She goes to look inside his mouth, but he is quick to avoid her.

ARTHUR It's nothing my dear, really.

SYLVIA *suddenly realises the cause of his toothache. Her eyes widen with surprise.*

SYLVIA Arthur Llewelyn Davies, have you been sneaking the boys' sweets?

ARTHUR *(scandalised)* Why, what a thing to ask!

SYLVIA You have! You devious man! I have half a mind to call your sons in here and expose you for the thief you are!

ARTHUR You wouldn't dare!

> *As* **SYLVIA** *rises,* **ARTHUR** *playfully grabs her around the waist and pulls her back to him.* **SYLVIA** *squeals with delight as she falls back into his arms.*

SYLVIA Alright then, it shall be our little secret. But let that toothache be a lesson to you.

ARTHUR I am forever in your debt.

> **SYLVIA** *looks at him with a sly smile spread across her lips.*

SYLVIA You are a wicked man, Arthur Llewelyn Davies.

ARTHUR I don't know what you're talking about, my dear.

> **ARTHUR** *kisses* **SYLVIA** *tenderly on the lips. As their kissing grows more passionate, the lights fade.*

2.2.

A couple of months later. Lights up on the parlour room of the **DAVIES** *household.* **ARTHUR** *is sitting in his chair, all alone in a very silent house. Everything is very still and the only sound we hear is the ticking of the grandfather clock. Finally, the door flings open and the entire room is suddenly abuzz with excited energy as* **SYLVIA** *(noticeably pregnant and holding* **PETER** *in her arms),* **BARRIE, MARY HODGSON** *and the boys come sweeping in.*

GEORGE We're famous, Father!

BARRIE *(still dumbstruck)* Splendid! Just splendid!

SYLVIA *(to* **ARTHUR***)* It was quite the success, dear. The audience loved it.

BARRIE An absolute smash!

SYLVIA *(looking lovingly at* **PETER***)* My darling Peter, tonight you are the talk of London.

By this point, **JACK** *has taken a half-eaten bag of sweets from his pocket and is now stuffing the remaining candies into his mouth.*

Oh Jack, darling, you'll be sick tomorrow if you go on eating your sweets like that.

JACK *(cheerily)* No, Mother. I'll be sick *tonight!*

With this, he continues to happily stuff the sweets into his mouth.

SYLVIA *moves to* **ARTHUR** *and gives him a kiss. He winces in pain.*

SYLVIA Oh my dear, you really must see the doctor about that. It's been months now.

ARTHUR Yes, yes, I know. I surrender. I shall go first thing tomorrow.

MARY *(not at all caught up in the excitement)* Alright, off to bed with you boys. I want you in bed with your teeth brushed and your hands washed before the kettle boils.

JACK Do we have to, Mary?

BARRIE Do as you're told, Jack. I'll be up in a moment to tell you boys a bedtime story.

MARY Hurry up now. I haven't got all night.

GEORGE You can't treat me that way! I'm the talk of London!

MARY Well if you're famous because of that play then so am I. So now we're even. Upstairs with you.

GEORGE But Mary, we were the inspiration for the whole play. You were only the inspiration for Nana! Being turned into a dog doesn't make you famous!

SYLVIA George!

MARY *(not missing a beat)* Well if I recall correctly, the title made no mention of a George. Or a Jack for that matter. I daresay it's your brother Peter who will be getting all the glory for this one. Now off to bed with you mongrels.

MARY *immediately realises what a poor choice of words she's just made.* GEORGE *picks up on it and begins to bark mockingly at* MARY. JACK *joins in the barking as* MARY *pushes them upstairs.* ARTHUR *silently helps to corral the boys, scooping* JACK *under his arm and carrying him up the stairs. Just before* MARY *goes, as the barking continues, she turns back and shoots a look at* BARRIE.

MARY Thanks ever so much, Mr. Barrie.

MARY *exits.* SYLVIA *and* BARRIE *burst into laughter.*

SYLVIA Really, Jimmy, did you have to make Nana a dog?

BARRIE Oh, she shouldn't take it so personally.

SYLVIA It really was a splendid evening. Your best success yet.

BARRIE I'm just glad to have it over with. Do you know, I was so afraid that no one would clap in response to Peter's plea to save Tink that I told the conductor, if no one clapped, the orchestra should drop their instruments and clap as if their lives depended on it. To think what a sorry sight that would have been!

SYLVIA laughs and looks lovingly at the infant in her arms.

SYLVIA And you, Peter. Did you enjoy it?

After a moment, SYLVIA looks up and sees BARRIE staring at her.

What is it?

BARRIE You really are the loveliest creature I've ever seen.

For a moment, they sit looking at each other. Then...

SYLVIA Please never say that again.

Lights fade.

2.3.

PETER *sits with* MARY *in Kensington Gardens, deep in conversation, with the statue looming behind them. It has been several months since their last meeting.*

MARY When your father finally went to the doctor about the pain in his cheek, they found it to be cancer. They operated straight away but the cancer had spread so quickly he lost half of his jaw. Your sweet mother was inconsolable. All she could say was, "They've spoilt my darling's face".[19] Just that, over and over again. "They've spoilt my darling's face". On his good days, we would bring you boys in to see him. Do you remember those visits?

PETER Only vaguely.

MARY He couldn't speak, but he would scribble little notes on a piece of paper telling you boys how much he loved you. Not long after that, he passed away.

PETER I feel so selfish for not remembering it better.

MARY One of the perks of being a child is that you're allowed to be unaware of the hardships happening around you.

MARY *senses that things have become very heavy and attempts to lighten the mood.*

Let's not talk of such things on a day like today. Tell me something wonderful.

PETER *(after a moment of consideration)* Have you heard the news about Uncle Jim? *(He gestures to the statue)* About Peter Pan?

MARY Yes, I read that he's giving all the rights to the children's hospital.

PETER A very kind gesture, isn't it?

MARY I trust it'll provide a significant amount of income for the hospital.

PETER Just don't think for a moment that he's doing it without hoping everyone will think he's somewhat of a saint.

MARY Even our kindest deeds sometimes have selfish motives.

PETER Well, I just think perhaps it would have been nice to have had a say in the matter. In a way, it's my money too, is it not?

MARY He'll find a way to repay you for it all. I'm certain of that.

PETER Yes well, I can't wait around forever can I? In fact, speaking of wonderful news, I've a bit of an announcement to make.

MARY Oh?

PETER I've recently decided to pursue a career in publishing. I'm going to start my own company.

MARY Well now, I was wondering how long it would take you to finally tell me.

PETER You mean you knew already? Barrie promised he wouldn't tell you!

MARY Barrie didn't tell me.

PETER Then who?

MARY *rummages through her handbag and produces a newspaper clipping. She hands it to him.*

(Reading) "Peter Pan Becomes Publisher". Splendid. Well, this will surely help people to take me seriously in my professional career.

MARY Oh, it's not all that bad. At least you're not forever associated with the thought of a slobbery dog.

They laugh. PETER *studies the article.*

PETER It's all very ridiculous, isn't it?

MARY Yes, quite.

PETER Why do they care what I do with my life?

MARY I can't say that I understand it myself.

PETER *(jovially)* Well, perhaps I'll become an alcoholic. Move to America and start robbing banks. Now that would give them something to write about!

As they laugh, a young female enters the scene. Though PETER *is immediately struck, the young* WOMAN *takes no notice of the odd pair occupying the bench and instead wanders over to the statue.*

MARY *(not noticing the girl)* You've always had quite a bit of your mother's rebellious spirit in you.

PETER *(distracted)* What? Oh, yes, of course.

MARY *sees that something has caught* PETER*'s eye and turns to look. She smiles when she realises what it is that has caught* PETER*'s attention.*

MARY Well, I'm afraid I must take my leave of you now.

PETER Oh Mary, please don't.

MARY Oh yes, I must. It's getting awfully late and you're not the only person I have to see today, you know. Besides, too much reminiscing never did anyone any good. We must always remember to live in the present.

They embrace.

Goodbye, my sweet Peter.

PETER Goodbye, Mary. And thank you again.

With this, MARY *exits.* PETER *slowly turns his attention to the young lady standing by the statue. He considers his course of action for a moment and then slowly and awkwardly moves towards her. Before he can reach her though, he is struck with doubt and makes a hasty retreat back to the bench. He sits, stands, then sits again. He then picks up the newspaper that is still lying on the bench and studies it for a moment.*

(to himself) Oh, grow up, Peter.

With this, he throws the paper to the ground, then rises and marches confidently up to the WOMAN. *She sees him and smiles politely. For a moment, he finds himself at a loss for words. Then, in a moment of panic, he turns his focus to the statue. The two stand somewhat awkwardly, obviously aware of the other's presence but neither one knowing what to say. Finally,* **PETER** *speaks.*

Splendid piece of work.

PEGGY Excuse me?

PETER I mean the —

He points to the statue.

PEGGY Oh. Yes.

Another awkward silence.

PETER Are you very fond of the story?

She considers the question for a moment before answering.

PEGGY When I was a little girl, yes. I think every little girl grows up hoping that one day Peter Pan will fly into their lives and take them away to Neverland.

PETER Is that so?

PEGGY When I first heard the story, I wanted so badly to be able to fly that I would sometimes take running leaps onto my bed, hoping desperately that I might take flight before my face hit the pillow... Quite silly, really.

PETER No, not at all.

Beat.

But as you grew older the story lost its magic?

PEGGY I suppose I just eventually saw the story for what it really is.

PETER Which is what?

PEGGY *(after a moment of thought)* That of a sad, lonely little boy.

PETER Why do you say that?

PEGGY Well... He has no family, no one who truly cares for him. He's been more or less forgotten by the world... And to never experience love. I mean, *true* love. The kind of love that only adults can really feel and appreciate. I think that's just…quite sad, really.

She suddenly becomes very aware of herself.

I'm sorry, I'm sure you don't want to hear my depressing opinion on the whole matter.

PETER Oh no, quite the contrary actually. Please, do go on.

She smiles shyly and then considers the statue for a moment.

PEGGY Well… The idea of someone never being able to truly grow up, of always being stuck in one place and never being able to move forward… That sounds awful to me.

Beat.

(Gesturing to the statue) And of course he's forever doomed to wear that little green dress, it would seem.

PETER *smiles.*

PETER I'm sorry, I didn't get your name.

PEGGY Margaret Ruthven, but everyone calls me Peggy. And you?

PETER My name is Peter.

Beat.

PEGGY *(smiling)* Well… It's nice to meet you, Peter.

Lights fade.

2.4.

Lights up. On one side of the stage we see **BARRIE**'s *study, and on the other side stands the Davies's parlour room.* **BARRIE** *is sitting at his desk, scribbling away. At the Davies household, a ten-year-old* **PETER** *sits at the piano.* **SYLVIA** *enters. She is dressed in black but still as lovely as ever.*

SYLVIA Are you ready, Peter?

PETER Yes, Mother.

SYLVIA *(sitting next to him)* Let's see what you've been practicing.

> **PETER** *begins to play. The piece flows quite nicely, but every now and again the flow is interrupted by an incorrect, fumbling note. As* **PETER** *plays, we see* **MARY ANSELL** *appear in the doorway of* **BARRIE**'s *study. She is dressed in a beautiful nightgown and her soft hair flows freely down her back. The music plays softly underneath the following scene. After a while, during the dialogue,* **SYLVIA** *joins in and the two begin to play a lovely duet.*

MARY ANSELL Will you come to bed?

BARRIE Not just yet, my dear, I'm very busy.

> **MARY** *walks over to him and kisses him tenderly on the forehead.*

MARY ANSELL Perhaps you might visit my room briefly before you turn in for the night?

BARRIE I'll be up quite late, my dear. I wouldn't want to wake you.

MARY ANSELL I wouldn't mind.

> *She leans over him and peers at what he's been writing. Slowly she begins kissing his neck.*

BARRIE Would you mind standing a ways off, dear?

MARY is hurt by this, but knows that pressing the matter further would be pointless.

MARY ANSELL Of course.

MARY reluctantly steps back as BARRIE continues his work. At length he lets out a small chuckle, obviously very pleased with what he has just written. MARY slowly turns to leave, but stops when she gets to the door. Still facing towards the hall, she speaks.

I'm having an affair.

BARRIE slowly stops what he is doing and looks up. He is dumbstruck and unsure of what to say.

BARRIE Oh.

MARY ANSELL *(turning to look at him)* I'm in love with him.

BARRIE I see.

MARY ANSELL Is that all you have to say?

BARRIE *(after some consideration)* You've given me up then?

MARY ANSELL You gave me up long ago, James. Don't pretend that this is all my fault.

BARRIE Mary, I love you.

MARY ANSELL Do you really believe that, James? No, you don't love me. You have *never* loved me.

BARRIE Don't be silly, of course I do.

MARY ANSELL No. There was a time when I believed those words. That's why I married you. I believed that you were capable of adult emotions, capable of love... But I see now that it is only your greatest pretend.

This remark cuts BARRIE to the core, mainly because he secretly fears that it is true.

BARRIE Mary —

MARY ANSELL You married me in a desperate attempt to prove that you were capable of loving a woman, of doing the things that real men do. And foolish me, I went along with it.

BARRIE You're being rather dramatic, don't you think?

MARY ANSELL Please don't assume that I think myself to be some grand figure of tragedy. No, I'm not tall enough. I'm just a woman who made a mistake.[20] I should never have married you.

BARRIE Then why did you?

MARY ANSELL Because I thought our love was mutual. And because I thought you were a genius. You are a genius. You're a genius at writing, you're a genius at games, but you are a failure at love.

After a pause, BARRIE *turns back to his work and speaks in a dismissing tone.*

BARRIE Lie down, my dear. You'll feel better after a rest and then we can talk rationally.

MARY ANSELL Didn't you even hear what I said? I'm having an affair. And I've fallen in love with him. Don't you even care?

Suddenly BARRIE *throws his work to the floor.*

BARRIE *(with force)* Of course I care! I am humiliated!

This reaction catches MARY *off guard. She has never seen this side of* BARRIE *and is unsure of what to say.*

MARY ANSELL It was never my intention to humiliate you.

BARRIE *(composing himself)* No, well... No matter. We can fix this. We'll pick up the pieces and start again. You will never see this man again and we'll work together to fix our marriage.

MARY ANSELL No, James. Love is not like a broken glass whose fragments you can pick up and piece back together. It's like fine wine that's been spilt all over the grass. You can't pick that up.[21]

BARRIE Please, Mary. I will give you all the love in my heart. I will love you with everything I have. Just, please, let us talk about this.

MARY ANSELL No, James. It's too late to talk of love and your giving it to me. *(A realisation)* I no longer want it.[22]

BARRIE Mary —

MARY ANSELL I want a divorce. Our love has brought me nothing but misery[23] and I demand to experience happiness at least once in my life.

Beat.

BARRIE I see.

MARY ANSELL I'm sorry to have hurt you.

BARRIE You should have come to me sooner. You should have tried harder before giving up on us like this.

MARY ANSELL I have been trying for years, James. I've tried on so many countless occasions to find a way into your heart and to pierce those reserves of yours. Sometimes I even feel as though I just might be succeeding. But then you close yourself off again and I am once more left outside in the cold.[24] I simply can't continue like this any longer.

BARRIE No, I won't accept this.

MARY ANSELL It's too late for that. I wanted this to work, James. But how could it when you're unable to love anyone but those boys? You don't know how to love a woman. How foolish of me to marry someone who is incapable of love. I'm sorry I ever asked such a thing of you. I realise now that you're still just a boy, and of course boys cannot love. And so I'm asking you to let me go. I want a divorce.

She goes to leave, but turns back to him when she reaches the door.

How cruel of me to ask a boy to love.

With that, she exits.

Suddenly, **SYLVIA** *stands.* **PETER** *stops playing the piano as* **SYLVIA** *takes a couple steps forward, then stops. Her face is pale and vacant. Her body appears to be suspended in the air, as though it were being held up by invisible strings. Then...*

SYLVIA Peter, get Mary. Quickly.

PETER, *confused, does as he is told and rushes from the room to fetch* **MARY.**

(In an almost inaudible whisper) Peter.

With this, **SYLVIA** *collapses.*

Blackout

2.5.

The Davies's household. Evening. **SYLVIA** *is in bed, looking pale and sickly.* **MARY HODGSON** *is sitting by her bedside, gently dabbing* **SYLVIA***'s forehead with a damp cloth. At length,* **BARRIE** *appears in the doorway.* **MARY** *rises and moves to him. They speak in low voices, so as to not let* **SYLVIA** *overhear.*

BARRIE How is she?

MARY The doctor said it's very bad. It's already spread and is now too near the heart for operation.[25]

BARRIE How long does she have?

MARY She may make it through the night, God willing, but she won't be able to hang on much longer. She can speak, but she's not very strong. She's asked that the boys not be allowed to see her like this.

BARRIE Of course... May I have a moment with her, please?

MARY nods and exits. **BARRIE** *goes to* **SYLVIA***'s side and takes her hand. Throughout the following exchange,* **SYLVIA** *speaks weakly and occasionally finds herself overcome by a sharp, painful sensation in her chest which leaves her gasping for air.*

My dear Sylvia.

SYLVIA It's so good of you to come.

BARRIE kisses her pale hand and presses it to his cheek.

Jimmy... Tell me what death is like.

BARRIE I can't say that I know. But I do know that Heaven will be a thousand times more beautiful once it has you in it.

SYLVIA *smiles at this but her smile quickly turns into a pained expression.*

SYLVIA Will you watch over my boys when I'm gone?

BARRIE Of course.

SYLVIA What a horrible thought, not being here to watch them grow up.

BARRIE Then I shall make you a promise. If you should go before me, I promise to write you a letter every year so that you may stay informed about all of the goings-on down here, including detailed descriptions of all the many wonderful things the boys have accomplished that year. I dare say your letters will make you the envy of every mother in Heaven.

SYLVIA Even when staring at death, you're still quite the poet.

BARRIE I admit my fault. Even as I proposed to Mary all those years ago, I foolishly thought about how it might read.[26]

Beat.

SYLVIA George told me what's happened. Are you angry with her?

BARRIE *(simply)* No. She was perfection.[27]

SYLVIA What will you do?

BARRIE *shrugs meekly.*

BARRIE Divorce. It's what she wishes, and I owe her at least that much.

SYLVIA You deserve happiness, Jimmy.

BARRIE Do you know, the only thing that has ever given me true joy is seeing *you* happy.

The sensation in SYLVIA*'s chest has grown increasingly worse and she lets out a small cry of pain.*

Sylvia, I have something to ask you. You need not answer right away. I only ask that you think about it with an open mind, and that you think about how good it might be for your happiness and the happiness of the boys. *Our* boys.

SYLVIA Of course, Jimmy. What is it that you want to ask?

BARRIE *(meekly at first, but then gathering courage)* Sylvia, for many years now I have stored within me a great deal of affection, with nobody to give it to. I tried in vain to give it to Mary, but I suppose a secret, cowardly part of me simply wasn't ready to part with it and so she was always unable to coax it from my hands. I have struggled lately to understand why that happened, but I now believe to know the cause. Perhaps she simply wasn't the one that my affections were meant for. Perhaps...perhaps there was someone else.

Beat.

I suppose what I'm trying to say is... If you would accept my affections, I should be very proud.

SYLVIA Jimmy, I don't understand.

BARRIE *(bravely, and most pathetically)* My dearest Sylvia...will you do me the honor of becoming my wife?

> **SYLVIA**, *taken aback, stares at him for a moment. Her face is filled with pity for this tragic boyish figure. After several moments of silence,* **SYLVIA** *speaks. She speaks not with love, but with pity, knowing full well that her answer is a promise which will never be fulfilled.*

SYLVIA *(in a hushed whisper)* Yes.

> **BARRIE** *breathes a sigh of pure elation and joy. He kisses* **SYLVIA**'s *hands, then rises.*

BARRIE I'll fetch Mary and the boys. We must share our news with them.

SYLVIA Jimmy, no —

> **SYLVIA** *reaches for him, but he is already gone. She sinks into her bed. Then suddenly, a sharp pain shoots through her chest. She grabs at it as she struggles to breathe. She begins coughing and gasping for air, but the pain only grows. Finally the pain begins to subside, but it is too late.* **SYLVIA** *grows limp and motionless. She is gone.*

> *At length, the door creaks open and* **PETER** *pokes his head in. He enters timidly, closing the door behind him.*

PETER Mother, will you come out and play with me?

When he doesn't receive a response, he walks slowly towards SYLVIA *and stops once he is halfway to her. He stands very still, staring at* SYLVIA's *motionless body.*

Are you still sleeping, Mother?

After a moment, BARRIE *and* MARY HODGSON *enter. They stop when they see* PETER.

MARY Peter? What are you doing in here?

BARRIE *(noticing that* SYLVIA *isn't moving)* Mary.

MARY Fetch the doctor! Quickly!

BARRIE *rushes out of the room as* MARY *hurries to* SYLVIA's *side.*

Sylvia?! Sylvia, can you hear me? Oh God, please —

The sound of chaos and alarm can be heard in the hallway. PETER *stands motionless as* MARY *frantically attempts to revive* SYLVIA. *She then dashes out of the room to fetch the doctor, leaving* PETER *alone.* PETER *remains perfectly still, like a serene ghost in the midst of the chaos, staring at* SYLVIA's *lifeless body.*

PETER Mother?

After a moment, lights fade to black.

End of Act Two

ACT THREE

3.1.

Lights up on **PETER**'s *study from the opening scene, only now it is before the move and therefore everything is in perfect order. The shelves are lined with books and the room is neat and tidy. Sunshine is streaming in through the windows.* **PEGGY**, *now* **PETER**'s *wife, is currently in the process of dusting the mantel of the fireplace. The sound of a door opening and closing is heard from offstage.*

PETER *(offstage)* Peggy?

PEGGY I'm in the study! Come here, I have something to show you!

PEGGY *quickly tidies the remaining clutter in the room. Then, unsure of where to put her duster, she makes for the desk, opens one of the drawers, and plops the duster inside. Just before she closes the drawer,* **PETER** *enters the room. He is a few years older than when we last saw him in the park with* **MARY**, *but has maintained his youthful good looks. He leans against the doorway and watches* **PEGGY** *with a smile.*

PETER Looking for something?

PEGGY *jumps a little.*

PEGGY No... Just doing a little spring cleaning.

PETER *(smiling)* Well, the next time you do your spring cleaning, don't complain to me when you can't remember where you've left your duster.

PEGGY *(with sweet mock innocence)* I would never forget such a thing.

PETER *moves to her and they embrace.*

How was work?

PETER Not the finest of days, but it's hardly worth speaking of.

PEGGY Did something happen?

PETER *sighs.*

PETER I lost a potential client today when the fellow realised who I was. He seemed to think that I knew nothing about publishing and was only there because the all-powerful J.M. Barrie had pulled some strings for me.

PEGGY Oh Peter, that's awful.

PETER Yes, well, can't really blame him, can we? I suppose the thought of Peter Pan handling my affairs would put me off as well. But let's not speak of it anymore. How was your day?

PEGGY Not much excitement really.

PETER You said you had something to show me?

PEGGY Yes, I almost forgot! I was doing some cleaning today and look what I found tucked away in one of those old trunks in the attic.

She reaches behind the desk and produces a box. As she tips the contents onto the desk, hundreds of photographs and letters come tumbling out.

PETER What are these?

PEGGY They must have belonged to your mother.

PETER *(flipping through the pile)* I've never seen these before.

PEGGY There are letters too. From Barrie, Michael... Everyone.

PETER *(smiling as he holds up a photograph)* This must have been taken during one of our summer holidays to Black Lake Cottage.

PEGGY *(holding up another photograph)* Look at this one. Is that you dressed as Peter Pan?

PETER No, that's Michael. That's the photo they used when they were creating the statue in Kensington Gardens.

PEGGY Why didn't they use you as the model?

PETER I don't know. I suppose they thought he was the handsomer of us Davies boys.

PEGGY Well now, I don't believe that for a moment.

She kisses him and they continue to sift through the pile.

Who took all of these photos? Your father?

PETER No, it was all Barrie. Everywhere we went, he always seemed to have a camera in his hand.

PEGGY *suddenly remembers something.*

PEGGY Speaking of Barrie...

PETER Yes?

PEGGY He rang earlier and said that he may stop by later.

PETER *(obviously annoyed)* Did he say what he wanted?

PEGGY Just some company I suppose. He spends most of his time sitting around that lonely flat of his.

PETER Yes, pining for my dead mother no doubt.

PEGGY Oh Peter, will you ever stop being angry about that?

PETER How can I? He claims that before her death he and my mother were engaged. It's a preposterous, damnable lie.

PEGGY He's just a sad, lonely man, Peter. Have pity on him.

PETER Pity?!

PEGGY *looks at him imploringly.*

PEGGY Peter... It'll only be for an hour or so. Surely you can be civil for an hour.

PETER *(unconvincingly)* I'll try.

PEGGY That's all I ask.

They kiss.

PETER Do you know, coming home to you is always the best part of my day.

PEGGY Well, now that I'm your wife you get to come home to me every day for the rest of our lives.

PETER Now, you see, that's wonderful for me. But what could you possibly get out of this arrangement?

PEGGY Well, believe it or not, I'm actually quite fond of you.

PETER Now that is something I will never understand.

They look sweetly at each other.

Dance with me?

PEGGY *smiles.* **PETER** *begins to hum a soft tune. As he hums, the two begin to dance. After a few moments,* **PEGGY** *looks up at* **PETER** *with a soft smile.*

PEGGY Peter?

PETER Yes, dear?

PEGGY I have another surprise for you.

PETER More boxes?

PEGGY No, not more boxes... This is a different kind of surprise.

PETER Oh?

PEGGY A very different kind.

PETER *begins to playfully pick up the pace and their slow dance morphs into more of a waltz.*

PETER *(playfully)* Let me guess. You've finally decided to take up smoking cigars, have you? Well, I knew it was only a matter of time.

PEGGY *(laughing)* No.

PETER I know, I know. You want us to move to Paris.

PEGGY No.

PETER You're considering taking up horse riding?

PEGGY No.

PETER You're having an affair?

PEGGY No.

PETER You're with child?

> **PEGGY** *is about to respond with another "no", but then stops herself.* **PETER** *laughs, but when he realises that* **PEGGY** *isn't saying anything, their dance slows to a halt.*

Peggy?

PEGGY It's true.

PETER What's true?

PEGGY We're going to have a baby.

> **PETER** *is silent. He appears to be in shock.*

Well, say something!

PETER Peggy, that's wonderful! Absolutely wonderful!

> **PETER** *is overcome with joy. He scoops* **PEGGY** *up into his arms and kisses her.*

A baby! You're positive?

> **PEGGY** *nods.*

We're going to have a family! Do you think it's a boy or a girl?

PEGGY I don't care what it is so long as it's ours.

PETER *(in delighted awe)* I'm going to be a father.

> *He lifts* **PEGGY** *up and spins her around. He then sets her gently down and places a hand lovingly on her stomach. They smile at each other, embrace, kiss, and embrace again. Then suddenly, the sound of a rather obnoxious bell interrupts their revelry. The two look at each other.*

PEGGY That must be Barrie.

PETER Impeccable timing as usual. Can't we just pretend that we're not at home?

PEGGY *(smiling)* No.

She kisses him on the cheek.

Now go. And be nice!

*As **PETER** exits, the lights fade.*

3.2.

Lights up on Kensington Gardens. **PETER** *is sitting on the bench and leaps to his feet when he sees* **MARY** *approaching. He rushes to her and lifts her off the ground.*

MARY *(laughing)* Well now, aren't you cheerful today!

PETER I have news, Mary.

MARY Do you now?

PETER You mean to tell me you don't know? For once my fame doesn't precede me?

MARY No, I know nothing. What is it?

PETER Peggy is expecting a baby.

MARY A baby? Oh how wonderful! Congratulations my sweet boy!

PETER We're absolutely over the moon about it. Of course it will be expensive to add a new member to our family, and, well, business hasn't been very good lately, but we'll find a way. Would you believe Peggy has already found a nurse? I think you'd like her. She's a young woman called Mildred. According to your tradition, I won't allow her to be called Nurse or Nanny or anything but just Mildred.[28]

MARY Well now, you just make sure that your children don't tie Mildred to a tree and I'm sure she'll be very grateful to you.

PETER *(laughing)* I'm sorry we were so horrible to you, Mary. But that reminds me. I wanted to show you something.

He pulls a photograph from his pocket and hands it to her.

MARY Lord, how young I was back then. And look, my favourite hat!

PETER Is that me you're holding?

MARY No, I believe that's Jack... I've never seen this photograph before. Where did you find it?

PETER Peggy found it hidden away in our attic. And not just this one. There are hundreds more. Letters too.

MARY I should like to see them.

PETER It's actually occurred to me to organise it all into some sort of cohesive collection, so that something of the Davies family history might be preserved.

MARY That sounds like quite the undertaking.

PETER Yes, but I think I'm up for it. Though the problem is that many of my old memories are streaky at best. I was wondering if perhaps you might be willing to help fill in the gaps.

MARY Oh, I —

PETER You have my word that you would never have to answer any questions that you don't feel comfortable with, or that bring up memories which are too painful to relive.

MARY Well I suppose I could try to help wherever I'm able.

PETER Dear, sweet Mary.

PETER *takes* **MARY***'s hand and kisses it lovingly.*

Do you think it's a boy or a girl?

Lights fade.

3.3.

Lights up on **PETER**'s *study.* **PETER** *is sitting at his desk sorting through a pile of paperwork while* **PEGGY** *busies herself about the room.*

PEGGY The weather was quite nice today, wasn't it?

PETER Yes, it was. Quite a relief after all the rain that we've had to endure this week.

PEGGY Did you manage to get out of the office for a bit and enjoy some fresh air?

PETER I'm afraid not. We were quite busy today.

PEGGY Well I simply couldn't stand being in such a stuffy house with such nice weather outside.

PETER Did you go to the park?

PEGGY Oh, no. I just wandered around the neighborhood a bit.

PETER *(with his nose still buried in his work)* That's nice.

PEGGY I don't think I do that often enough. I had almost forgotten what lovely houses are just around the corner from ours.

PETER Yes, I suppose.

PEGGY In fact, I got to talking with one of our neighbors and she mentioned that a few of the houses will actually be vacant quite soon.

PETER *(looking up)* Did you happen to stop by Barrie's while you were out and pick up that book he wanted to lend me?

PEGGY No, I suppose it slipped my mind. I'll get it first thing tomorrow.

PETER Thank you, dear. That's most kind of you.

For a moment, they continue with their work in silence. Then **PEGGY**, *unable to resist, pipes in again.*

PEGGY Those houses really are quite spectacular.

PETER *(reluctantly)* Yes, quite.

PEGGY Perhaps we could take a look at them sometime? Just to get an idea of what's available at the moment.

PETER Peggy, I thought I'd made it very clear that I wasn't interested in discussing such things.

PEGGY I just think it would be wise for us to start considering the idea of investing in a larger house.

PETER We can't afford it right now.

PEGGY But you can't possibly expect the three of us to stay here.

PETER Of course I can. This place is perfectly suitable for our needs.

PEGGY It has been, yes. But not anymore. Not with a baby on the way. It's much too small for three people to live in comfortably. And what about later, when there are more children? It's absurd to think we could stay here. I think we should move now, before the baby comes.

PETER We don't have the money for it.

PEGGY Ask Barrie. He'd help you.

PETER I don't want his help.

PEGGY I know you don't like to ask him for favours, but what other choice do we have?

PETER There must be something else we can do.

PEGGY Well... Why don't you ask your cousin Daphne? The Du Mauriers have plenty of money to go around. And, after all, you're family.

PETER I'd rather the Du Mauriers not know about our current financial troubles.

PEGGY I hardly think Daphne would think twice about it.

PETER It would still be humiliating for me, Peggy.

PEGGY Well, if you can't ask your own family for help then who *can* you ask?

PETER *says nothing.*

Peter, why do you continually refuse to reach out to people for help? We can't do this on our own.

PETER I'll find a way.

PEGGY How?

PETER Trust me with this, Peggy.

PEGGY Please, Peter, just ask Barrie. He'd be more than happy to help us. I know you don't want to be indebted to him, but —

PETER Yes, you're right.

PEGGY But Peter, he *is* your adopted father. Surely it wouldn't be out of place to ask your own father —

PETER *(firmly)* He is *not* my father.

PEGGY No, I know. I only meant —

PETER Can't it just wait? When he dies my inheritance will be such that we'll be set for life, and we can use that money to buy ourselves a beautiful new home. But I'd rather wait until then.

PEGGY And in the meantime?

PETER We'll stay here.

PEGGY You know that's not an option.

PETER Well then I'll just have to get us the money some other way. *Without* having to ask Barrie.

PEGGY But Peter, *how?*

PETER Peggy, just trust me. You really shouldn't be concerning yourself with such matters anyway. I'll make it work. I promise.

PEGGY But Peter —

PETER Please don't worry your head about it anymore. You just find your dream home and then let me take care of the rest.

PEGGY *studies him for a moment.*

PEGGY Do you really mean that?

PETER I only want to see you happy. You can start looking as soon as you wish.

PEGGY You're positive about this?

PETER Yes. Now please, no more on the subject.

PEGGY Oh, thank you! You won't regret it, I promise.

She kisses him gingerly on the cheek.

You're a wonderful husband.

PETER Do you know, it makes everything worth it just to hear you say that.

PEGGY Shall I make us some tea?

PETER Yes, that'd be lovely, dear.

PEGGY *exits. Once she is gone,* **PETER** *drops the charade and begins to pace about the room. He looks worried and tired. As he paces, the lights fade.*

3.4.

Lights up on **PETER** *and* **MARY** *in Kensington Gardens.*
PETER *sits with a notebook in his lap, scribbling away as*
MARY *speaks.*

MARY *(studying a photograph)* That's Charles Frohman, Barrie's producer. There was no bigger supporter of *Peter Pan* than Charles Frohman. Even when everyone else was convinced that the play was going to be a complete flop, Mr. Frohman bet his life savings against them. Such a lovely man. And stubborn till the bitter end.

PETER What happened?

MARY He drowned when his ship bound for America was torpedoed. He was offered a spot in one of the lifeboats but the story goes that he turned it down, saying something along the lines of "To die will be an awfully big adventure".[29]

PETER *(under his breath)* Bloody fool.

Beat.

I had never heard that story.

MARY Yes, I made sure of that. You were too young at the time to hear such awful tales.

PETER Do you know, the older I get, the more I realise how much you did for us. How unruly and ungrateful we must have seemed.

MARY It was my job. I just wanted to protect you boys from life's harsh realities.

PETER How I wish one could think more of the happy beginnings and less of the melancholy ends.[30] When reflecting back on all the death and misery that descended on our happy family, one can become quite depressed.

MARY We must not allow ourselves to dwell on the unhappy events of the past.

PETER I know it might seem unfair of me, but I can't help but want to blame Barrie for it all. How different life would have been without him.

MARY We all have our battles, Peter. But that's no one's fault, that's just life. And I may not be the greatest fan of his, but I will say that Barrie has certainly had to endure his fair share of hardships.

PETER (*doubtfully*) Such as?

MARY You mean aside from his humiliating and very public divorce? Did anyone ever tell you the story of his sister's fiancé?

PETER I can't recall.

MARY His favorite sister, Maggie, was getting married, and as a wedding present Barrie bought her fiancé a beautiful horse. Then, a few days before the wedding, Maggie's fiance was out riding when something spooked the horse. It reared on its hind legs and threw the young man to the ground. He died almost instantly.

PETER *is silent.*

Everyone who had come to Scotland to celebrate the young man's marriage found themselves attending his funeral... Then there was Barrie's agent who shot himself in Switzerland.

Beat.

PETER Yes, well, on that cheery note, I suppose I should tell you that I've settled on a title for my collection of letters and photographs. I shall call it The Morgue. It just seemed like quite a fitting title for such a depressing collection.

MARY Peter, you do know that you don't have to continue with this project if it gets to be too much for you. The past is often a sad and meaningless place to dwell.

PETER Thank you, Mary. But no, I'm interested in it. Truly. Interested to find out things that happened in my boyhood which I never knew about. Things that were happening right in front of me. To be honest, I've been a little surprised, and rather disgusted too, to find how little I can have felt at the time, thanks to dwelling in the selfish and separate world of childhood. Though the delayed effect those sad events had on me is another matter, as I now seem to possess a kind of innate and circumstantial gloom.[31] For indeed, the more one learns of those sad days, the sadder the tale becomes... Still, *(he smiles a somewhat forced smile)* I think it's all worth preserving.[32]

He closes the notebook and tucks it into his pocket.

Lights fade.

3.5.

Lights up on **PETER**'s *study. The shades are mostly drawn but some mid-afternoon sunlight still peeks through.* **PEGGY** *(whose pregnancy is now starting to show) and* **PETER** *are sitting on the floor with the photographs and letters that will make up the contents of* **PETER**'s *morgue spread in front of them. As they sort through the pile, a smile spreads across* **PEGGY**'s *face and she lets out a small giggle.*

PETER What's so funny?

PEGGY Nothing. Just a thought I had... No matter.

They continue sorting. **PEGGY** *looks at* **PETER** *with a slight smirk on her face, as though she's hiding an amusing secret.*

I never asked, how was your day?

PETER Quite uneventful really.

PEGGY I see.

PETER And you?

PEGGY Oh it wasn't very exciting. Though I read an interesting article in the newspaper while I was drinking my tea.

PETER Oh?

PEGGY In fact, I wanted to show it to you.

She stands and fetches a newspaper off of the side table. She flips to an earmarked page and hands it to **PETER**. **PETER** *reads:*

PETER "Peter Pan fined for speeding".

PEGGY *can no longer contain her laugher. She falls to the ground in a giggly heap.*

PEGGY I'm sorry to laugh, Peter.

PETER No, it's right that you do. How ridiculous. It seems that nothing escapes their watchful eyes. Though this time I daresay it was my own fault... I'm sorry for not telling you, dear.

PEGGY Well, just don't do it again.

PETER You have my word.

He kisses her, then crumples up the newspaper and playfully throws it into the fireplace. They continue sorting, but **PEGGY***'s mind is still on the newspaper. After a moment, she speaks.*

PEGGY Peter... How do you know that Barrie named Peter Pan after you?

PETER *is a bit taken aback by this.*

PETER What do you mean?

PEGGY Well, Peter is quite a common name. I mean, did Barrie ever actually tell you that he had named Peter Pan after you?

PETER Well, no, I suppose he never formally mentioned it. But of course he named him after me.

PEGGY But what if you're wrong? Wouldn't that be such a relief?

PETER No, I'm quite sure of it.

PEGGY Well perhaps we should ask him.

PETER No, I don't think so.

PEGGY But what if —

PETER *(firmly)* Peggy, I really don't wish to continue with this conversation.

PEGGY *is caught off guard by* **PETER***'s reaction to the subject.*

PEGGY Yes, of course. We'll forget I ever mentioned it.

They continue to sort. At length, **PEGGY** *holds up a photograph.*

Look at this one of your mother. She looks like an angel. Is that Michael and Jack she's sitting with?

PETER *examines the photo.*

PETER No, that's Michael and George. It was probably taken just before George headed off to Eton.

PEGGY I should have liked to have met them.

PETER I can't say I'm all that sorry that you never met my brothers. They were both far more handsome than me. I'm certain you would have fallen in love with one of them and left me in a heartbeat.

PEGGY I very much doubt that. After all, I didn't fall in love with Jack when I met him, did I?

PETER Well now, I don't mean to pick favorites, but Jack's good looks couldn't hold a candle to the likes of Michael and George.

PEGGY *laughs. They continue sorting.*

PEGGY Do you miss them?

PETER Every day.

PEGGY Was Barrie close to them?

PETER Very much so. George was the first one of us that he met and Barrie made no attempt to hide the fact that George was his favorite. But when George got older and stopped believing in all the fairy stories, Barrie turned to Michael. Michael always had quite the imagination so he fell right under his spell... Then one day Barrie was coming up the path to his home when a reporter stopped him and asked what his feelings were when he heard about the drowning... He had no idea what the reporter was talking about. The news of Michael's death hadn't reached him yet.

PEGGY How awful.

PETER Do you know, I've always found it curious that no matter how old I get or how grey my hair becomes, Michael will forever be a boy of twenty... Lord knows what happened that day. He just went right into that pond and never came back out. Some said that it was an accidental drowning, while others said it was suicide. In the end, I think you have to believe whatever helps you sleep. For me, I couldn't be at peace thinking that it was all just a freak accident. I had to believe it was a choice Michael had made... Did you know he was terrified of water?

PEGGY Really?

PETER All his life. Absolutely petrified. He was plagued with terrible nightmares from his boyhood up through his days at Eton. And no matter how hard he tried to overcome his fear of water, he just couldn't shake it.

PEGGY And yet he died by drowning?

PETER I've heard it said before that when you're afraid of something, be it water or guns or fire, it's because deep down in your gut, something in you knows that that's how you're going to die.

After a moment of stillness, suddenly and very loudly, the telephone rings. This startles them both, causing them to jump a little. As they compose themselves and chuckle at their silliness, PEGGY rises and answers the telephone.

PEGGY Hello?...Yes, this is she... Hello, Cynthia — Oh, I see... Yes, of course... We'll be there shortly... Of course. Thank you for calling us.

She hangs up.

PETER What is it?

PEGGY That was Barrie's secretary... Peter, Barrie passed away this morning.

As they look at each other, the lights fade.

3.6.

Lights up on the bench in Kensington Gardens on a very cold, overcast day. It is the day of **J.M. BARRIE***'s funeral. For several moments, the stage is bare and silent. At length,* **PETER** *stumbles in and sits on the bench. He is dressed in a black suit. For a moment he sits completely still, lost in his thoughts. Then he notices a newspaper lying at his feet. He picks it up and reads the headline. It is obviously to do with* **BARRIE***'s death.*

PETER *(bitterly, sarcastically)* Splendid.

He lets the paper fall to the ground. At length, **MARY HODGSON** *enters. She is also dressed in black.*

MARY Peter? I thought I might find you here. Everyone is looking for you.

For a moment, **PETER** *is silent. Then...*

PETER Furniture.

MARY I don't follow.

PETER Furniture. He left me his furniture. His dingy, old furniture.

MARY I see.

PETER Did you hear who he left nearly all of his money to? Along with the rights to all of his published works?

MARY Peter —

PETER His secretary.

MARY Peter, I'm sorry. I don't know what to say.

Beat.

PETER What was that he said in his book?

For a moment he searches for the words. Then...

"There never was a simpler, happier family until the coming of Peter Pan".[33]

MARY Peter...

PETER I didn't ask to be part of his story, Mary.

MARY I know.

PETER Why Peter? Why couldn't he have named him George or Michael or Jack?

MARY I suppose he thought that naming his creation after you was a kind of gift.

PETER Rather a curse.

MARY Peter, it's only a name. What's in a name?

This comment strikes a deep chord in **PETER**.

PETER What's in a name? My God what isn't? If that perennially juvenile lead, if that boy so fatally committed to an arrestation of his development, had only been dubbed George, or Jack, or Michael, or Nicholas, what miseries would have been spared me![34]

Beat. **PETER** *struggles to compose himself.*

Forgive me, Mary. I'm not myself today.

PETER, *unable to look* **MARY** *in the eye, turns his solemn gaze to his aging hands as he speaks.*

Peggy has found a house. A beautiful house that she wants to raise our family in.

MARY Well that's wonderful, Peter.

PETER We can't afford it. Business has been very poor lately. I haven't had the heart to tell her. I thought that once Barrie passed away, my inheritance would be such that we could buy several houses if we so desired. But as it turns out, I have nothing...

For a moment, they are both silent. **PETER** *continues to stare blankly at his hands for a long while, mourning* *the man that he feels he has failed to become. At length, he looks up at* **MARY** *with the eyes of a sad, lonely little boy.*

What am I to do, Mary?

MARY, *always the one with the answers, now finds herself at a loss for words. She gently takes* **PETER***'s hand and clasps it between her own. As the two figures sit defeated on the bench, the lights begin to fade.*

End of Act Three

ACT FOUR

4.1.

Several months have passed. A very pregnant **PEGGY** *sits in the study with the curtains partially drawn. The room is beginning to fill with moving boxes and several books have been removed from their shelves. The contents of the morgue have been moved to a heap on top of the desk. The sound of a door opening and closing is heard offstage. At length,* **PETER** *enters the study, carrying a briefcase in his hand. He's in a temperamental mood.*

PEGGY How was work?

PETER *sits at the desk and begins pulling various papers from his briefcase.*

PETER *(flatly)* It was uneventful.

PEGGY Did you see Mary today?

PETER Yes, briefly.

PEGGY Did you tell her that the baby is due any day now?

PETER No, I didn't think to mention it.

PEGGY Well surely she'll be thrilled to hear that. Though it must be somewhat difficult to see the boy that you helped raise grow up and have a family of his own.

PETER *continues to focus on his paperwork.*

I felt the baby kick today. It nearly scared me half to death.

PETER *(growing increasingly agitated)* Please dear, I can't focus on my work if you insist on going on like this.

PEGGY *(gently)* You work too hard.

PETER *says nothing.*

I think you're putting too much pressure on yourself lately.

PETER You don't understand. I have to.

PEGGY But why?

PETER Because if I fail, the whole world will say, "Look, Barrie was right about him. He'll always be just a poor little boy trying desperately to pose as a man".

PEGGY Peter, trust me, everything is going to be okay.

PETER How can you know?

PEGGY You can't. But sometimes you just have to take a leap of faith.

PETER *(doubtfully)* A leap of faith?

PEGGY Yes.

PETER I lost my wings long ago, Peggy.

Beat.

PEGGY *(softly)* Fine. I'll say no more about it then... Shall I make us some tea?

No response. **PEGGY** *tries again to reach him.*

Peter, would you like me to make some tea?

PETER *(flatly)* Whatever you wish, dear.

PEGGY *is confused by* **PETER***'s coldness and unsure of how to proceed. She decides not to pester him further and instead leaves the room. After a moment,* **PETER** *pushes his paperwork aside and picks up a newspaper lying on the desk. He opens it and begins to casually peruse the pages. After a couple of turns, he comes to a page which has had a rather large article cut out of it, leaving an awkward gaping hole. Knowing it must have been an article about himself which* **PEGGY** *thought best to remove, he drops the paper in the bin and rubs his face with his hands. He then turns his attention to the photographs on the table. Compiling* *the morgue has now become an almost crippling task for him. It is something which pains him to do, yet something which he cannot seem to put aside. At length,* **PEGGY** *enters carrying a nicely arranged tray containing two cups and saucers and a selection of biscuits. She says nothing as she places the tray gently in front of* **PETER**.

I'd prefer to sit alone if you don't mind.

PEGGY *is hurt by this but says nothing. She removes her teacup from the tray and leaves the room.* **PETER** *stares at the tray for a moment and then pushes it away. He then opens a drawer and pulls out a bottle of gin. He tips a bit of it into his teacup and picks up a photograph. As he stares intently at the photograph, he takes a swig of the gin. Suddenly, a pained cry from* **PEGGY** *is heard in the other room, accompanied by the sound of shattering glass.* **PETER** *jumps to his feet.*

Peggy?

PEGGY *appears in the doorway, with her hand on her stomach. Her expression is one of panic and confusion.*

PEGGY Something is wrong.

Lights snap to black.

4.2.

A gloomy, overcast day. MARY *waits by the bench in Kensington Gardens. She seems nervous and impatient. At length,* PETER *enters. He appears distracted and deflated.*

PETER I'm sorry to have kept you waiting, Mary.

MARY *(with concern)* Don't be silly. How is she?

PETER She's recovering but will need to stay in the hospital for another week or so. Her parents are with her now.

MARY And the baby?

PETER He's going to be alright. We're incredibly grateful to the doctors for everything they've done for us.

MARY Oh Peter, that's wonderful news. I was so worried when I heard Peggy had taken ill.

They sit for a moment.

(Attempting to lighten the mood) Well now you must tell me all about the little one. What is he like?

PETER *(reluctantly)* Oh, well... He's all smiles. It seems he has inherited his mother's sunny disposition.

MARY That's good to hear. And Peggy? She's recovering nicely?

PETER Oh...yes.

Beat. MARY *studies* PETER'*s face.*

MARY What is it?

PETER *(evasively)* What do you mean?

MARY I've known you since you were a baby. I can tell when you're keeping something from me.

After a moment of hesitation, PETER *takes a deep breath and speaks.*

PETER Well, actually... You see Mary, it seems that a bit of a cloud has descended over our family.

MARY Oh, Peter, is it the baby?

PETER No... Well, maybe... You see, there were some complications during the delivery. The doctors ran a few tests, and...well...it seems Peggy is ill.

MARY Ill?

PETER The doctors have discovered that she has Huntington's Disease.

Beat.

MARY I see. Is it very serious?

PETER Yes, I'm afraid so. It's a nasty disorder which leads to dementia and all sorts of terrors. It's a horrible way to go, Mary.

MARY Oh Peter, I'm so sorry.

PETER I've been absolutely awful to her lately, Mary. I've been terrible to live with.

MARY Peter, you didn't know. And you've been under a lot of stress lately. I'm sure she understands.

PETER *shakes his head.*

PETER There's more.

MARY Oh?

PETER The doctors have told us that there's a fifty percent chance that our son has inherited the disease. And any future offspring that we may have will be in danger of inheriting it as well.

MARY Peter... I don't know what to say. I'm so sorry.

Beat. PETER *stares at his hands for a moment before speaking.*

PETER I'm going to sell the business. We'll need the money to pay for medical bills. I want Peggy to have the best care London can offer. Please don't mention it to her. I thought it best that I wait to tell her.

MARY Yes, of course... Peter, I know that things look bleak now, but you have to believe that it's only temporary. Things will get better. Perhaps the disease won't affect Peggy as terribly as it has others.

PETER Thank you, Mary. How I wish I could believe that...but I seem to have lost the ability to believe in such fairy stories.

MARY *takes* PETER's *hand and encloses it between her own. For a moment they sit completely still. Then suddenly* PETER *becomes self-conscious. He composes himself and pats* MARY's *hand gently.*

Forgive me, Mary. I'm letting my emotions get the better of me.

MARY One could hardly blame you for that, Peter.

PETER I think I just need a moment alone, if you don't mind.

MARY Do you really think you should be alone right now? Wouldn't you rather have some company?

PETER I quite appreciate your concern, Mary, but I just need a moment to compose myself is all.

MARY *(doubtfully)* Well if that's what you really think you need...

PETER It is. I'll ring you very soon. I promise.

MARY Please do. And give my love to Peggy.

PETER I will.

MARY *gets up to leave. Just before she goes, she turns back to* PETER.

MARY You're sure that you want to be alone?

PETER *(with attempted cheer)* Yes, of course. I'll be fine, dear Mary. Don't you worry about me.

MARY *exits and* PETER *is left alone. For a moment he remains on the bench, then stands and moves to the Peter Pan statue. As he stands motionless, staring at the statue, the lights begin to change. As this happens,* PEGGY *appears and moves to* PETER's *side, and we slowly find ourselves transported back to scene 2.3.*

4.3.

Flashback to scene 2.3.

PEGGY The idea of someone never being able to truly grow up, of always being stuck in one place and never being able to move forward... That sounds awful to me.

Beat.

(Gesturing to the statue) And of course he's forever doomed to wear that little green dress, it would seem.

PETER *(smiling)* I'm sorry, I didn't get your name.

PEGGY Margaret Ruthven, but everyone calls me Peggy. And you?

PETER My name is Peter.

Beat.

PEGGY *(smiling)* Well... It's nice to meet you, Peter... And what do you make of the statue then?

PETER *(after a considered pause)* I think he's terribly arrogant.

PEGGY Oh?

PETER Like he has it all figured out. Like you could throw anything at him and he'd always come out victorious.

PEGGY Well, I suppose we all feel that way when we're young.

PETER Yes, I suppose we do, don't we?

They continue to stare at the statue.

Do you have any idea what it's like to have a constant shadow, Miss. Ruthven?

PEGGY Yes, I do, actually.

PETER *is surprised by this answer.*

76

I have a twin sister, you see.

PETER You mean to say there's two of you?

PEGGY Exactly. Try as I might, I can never truly be my own person, because in a sense, we are two halves of the same person. And unfortunately for me, she's always been considered the prettier half.

PETER Now that I simply don't believe. I don't think there's anyone on this earth more beautiful than you.

Beat.

PEGGY *(blushing)* That's kind of you to say.

PETER *(mortified)* I'm sorry, that was terribly blunt of me.

PEGGY No, really —

PETER I can't believe I've just said such a thing —

PEGGY It's fine, really.

PETER You must think me an overconfident fool. Please, let us start over again.

Beat.

Please?

PEGGY *(smiling)* If that's what you wish.

PETER *smiles.*

PETER Stay here.

PETER *quickly moves to the bench and gestures to a giggling* PEGGY *to look away. He then performs a silly routine of standing, sitting and then standing again as* PEGGY *sneaks amused glances in his direction. At length, he makes his way over to her.*

(Gesturing to the statue) Splendid piece of work.

Beat. A smile spread across PEGGY's *lips.*

PEGGY You know, I couldn't agree more.

Lights fade to black.

4.4.

PETER's *study. About a month has passed since the last
scene in the park with* MARY. *The room is now as it was
at the top of the play, filled with moving boxes and piles of
old books. It is evening and only one or two of the lamps
are lit, making the room dark and gloomy. The lighting
is also such that the player's shadows appear larger than
life and move with great mischief along the walls.* PEGGY,
*no longer pregnant and looking much frailer than the last
time we saw her, is sat at the desk. She is staring intently
at the contents of the morgue, as though trying to unlock
the mystery that is her husband. A nearly empty bottle of
gin is perched on the corner of the desk. At length, we hear a
door open and close.* PETER *enters the room.*

PEGGY *(moving to him)* Where have you been?

PETER Please, Peggy, not today.

PEGGY I called the office and they said you didn't come in this
morning.

PETER *avoids her gaze.*

PETER Where's the baby?

PEGGY My parents took him for the night. They thought we might
like some time alone together.

PETER *says nothing.*

Peter, please answer me. Where have you been?

PETER I took a personal day to clear my head. That's all.

PEGGY You know we can't afford for you to be taking personal
days.

PETER *is silent.*

Have you been drinking?

Again, PETER *says nothing.*

Of course you have. What a silly question... Peter, this is
absurd. Why won't you just talk to me?

PETER I don't know how anymore.

PEGGY Yes, I've gathered that... Why?

PETER You wouldn't understand.

PEGGY Try me.

> **PETER** *tries to speak, but is unable to find an adequate way of putting into words all that he is feeling. After a moment of struggle,* **PEGGY** *chimes in.*

Well, you're right. I don't understand.

PETER Peggy, please. Let's discuss this later. Now just isn't a good time.

PEGGY It's never a good time for you, Peter.

> **PETER** *says nothing.*

I'm ill, Peter.

PETER Yes, I'm very aware of that.

PEGGY Well don't you think that we should talk about it?

PETER Yes, of course, but... I can't.

PEGGY Believe me, it's not easy for me either. But there are things that we need to discuss.

PETER Peggy, please... I just... I can't face such a conversation right now.

> **PETER** *moves to the desk.* **PEGGY** *watches as he pours himself a glass of gin.*

PEGGY Well then, you're not the man I thought you were. You're just a damn coward.

PETER Yes, I am. I'm a coward and a failure, Peggy. And the sooner you accept that fact, the better off we'll both be.

> **PETER**, *considering the conversation closed, reaches for one of the photographs on the desk.* **PEGGY** *lunges at him and knocks the photograph from his hand. She then grabs his face and forces him to look at her.*

PEGGY Talk to me!

PETER *yanks her arm away and the two begin to struggle.*

PETER Stop this!

PEGGY *finally manages to struggle free of* PETER*'s grasp.*
She pushes him away violently.

PEGGY You pathetic excuse for a father!

This cuts PETER *deeply.*

PETER Please, don't.

Beat.

PEGGY What is it you want, Peter?

For a moment, PETER, *utterly exhausted and broken,*
struggles to find the right words. Then...

PETER I just want to forget myself.

Beat.

PEGGY Believe me, I feel it too. You think I'm not angry with the
world? With God? You think I'm not scared? Of course I am.
But we need to talk about it because bottling it up won't do
either of us any good. Peter, please. Just talk to me.

PETER *(suddenly becoming very defensive)* I don't want to talk to
you.

PEGGY Well that's too bad because I'm your wife. We're in this
together. I'm a part of your life whether you like it or not.

PETER *(exploding)* Well maybe I made a mistake in marrying you!
Maybe I should have just been alone. Maybe I would have been
happier that way. Without you. Without anyone. All I want
right now is to just be left alone!

PEGGY *is shocked to the core by this outburst. For a moment*
she stands frozen, staring at him in disbelief. Then...

PEGGY Fine then, be alone. I don't want to be around you anyway.
You're not the man I married. You're just a worthless drunk.

PETER goes to his desk and picks up the bottle of gin. He looks at PEGGY as he takes a defiant swig straight from the bottle. PEGGY stares at him with great disappointment.

They were right, you know. You really are just a boy trying desperately to pose as a man. And foolish me, I believed that you would become the kind of man, the kind of husband and father, who could handle any hardships that were thrown his way. I see now that I was wrong about you... Poor Peter, he'll always be just a silly, lonely little boy.

This comment cuts PETER to the core. PEGGY goes to leave, but just before she exits, PETER cries out to her.

PETER Peggy, please!

PEGGY *stops.*

Beat.

You know I didn't mean it.

PEGGY No, I don't.

PETER *(softly)* Please. Forgive me.

He struggles to hold back his tears.

Peggy, I'm afraid. I'm afraid of everything. The only thing keeping me sane is you. You're the only good thing I have left. I can't lose you.

PEGGY *studies him carefully.*

PEGGY What is it you want, Peter?

PETER considers this question carefully. He then looks at PEGGY with imploring, pleading eyes and extends his hand to her.

PETER Dance with me?

PEGGY looks at PETER's outstretched hand with great pain and longing. Finally, she speaks...

PEGGY No, Peter. Real life isn't like that. You can't fix everything with a smile and some fairy dust. It's time to grow up.

With this, she exits.

For a moment, **PETER** *is still. Then he slowly moves to his desk and sinks heavily into his chair. He stares blankly at the photographs and letters lying in front of him. At length,* **PETER** *opens a drawer and pulls out another bottle of gin. He takes a swig and then moves to put the bottle back in the drawer. This time, however, something at the back of the drawer catches his eye. He pulls it out and examines it. It is* **PEGGY**'s *duster. At first a slight smile spreads across his lips, but as he turns the object over in his hands, his expression becomes one of extreme sadness. At length, he places the duster back in the drawer and stares at the photographs in front of him. For a moment he is motionless and all is very silent. Then the scene begins to unfold as it did at the beginning of the play.* **PETER** *rises and begins to pace about the room, occasionally returning to the desk to pick up a photograph, study it, and then throw it back into the pile of old memories. As he paces, he seems to grow more and more agitated. At length, he picks up one of the empty boxes from the floor and sweeps all of the photographs and letters into it. He then pulls a packet of matches from his pocket. As he strikes a match, his weary face is illuminated. After a brief pause,* **PETER** *tosses the match into the box and watches for a moment as the flames consume the old photographs and letters. He then places the box in the fireplace. As the fire builds, the shadows on the wall become sharper and more sinister.* **PETER** *stands still for a moment, watching as all the reminders of his past are consumed by the flames. He then fetches his hat and overcoat and moves to the door. He takes one last look at the fire, then exits.*

Lights fade.

4.5.

*Lights up. A rainy platform at Sloane Square Station.
A projection flickers on the walls of the stage and we are
transported back to the lavish New Year's Eve dinner
party on December 31, 1897. The footage appears darker
and more dreamlike than when we first saw the scene,
as the moment now exists only in* PETER'*s imagination.
The projection flickers and stutters, like an old tape that's
been scratched and neglected. Occasionally it flickers out
altogether, thus allowing some of the onstage action to
unfold before it flickers back into life again. As* SYLVIA
and BARRIE *speak, the* PETER *from the previous scene
enters and stands calmly on the platform. Playing faintly
beneath the following exchange is the music that* SYLVIA
and PETER *played together in scene 2.4.*

SYLVIA And how do you choose the subject on which you write
about?

BARRIE I write about whatever intrigues me. Desert islands,
shipwrecks. Happiest is he who writes of adventure.

SYLVIA It sounds like something that my boys would enjoy. They're
always playing at pirates and indians. Many a time have I had
to rescue their poor nursemaid after they've taken her prisoner
and tied her to a tree.

*At the station, the sound of rattling train tracks and a
distant flickering light within the tunnel indicates an
approaching train.* PETER *watches as the train bursts into
the station and then quickly comes to a stop. The doors of
the train open but* PETER *remains stationary. At length,
the doors close and the train departs.*

SYLVIA *and* BARRIE'*s conversation continues. During
the exchange,* PETER *takes a seat on a nearby bench. He
pulls a newspaper clipping from his pocket and reads. It*

is an article containing the headline "Peter Pan Becomes a Father." PETER stares at it.

BARRIE Tell me, how old are your sons?

SYLVIA George is eleven, Jack is ten, and Peter is just a babe.

BARRIE Ah, all under twelve. How splendid. Nothing that happens after we are twelve matters very much. If you ask me, the end of boyhood is the end of a life worth living.

SYLVIA Do you really believe that, Mr. Barrie?

BARRIE Oh absolutely. Do you know what genius is, Mrs. Davies? It is the power to be a boy again at will.

A gentle rattling is once again heard coming from the tracks, accompanied by a faint flickering light within the tunnel, indicating the approaching arrival of a second train. PETER stands and moves calmly to the edge of the platform. His expression is not one of anger or despair, but rather that of a sad little boy forced to walk the plank by his bullying brothers.

SYLVIA But surely the end of boyhood isn't the end of a life worth living. Why, think of all the adventures that are still ahead of them: University, marriage, children, a career.

BARRIE Yes but in boyhood, you are blissfully unaware. The world is a magical place where nothing can touch you or bring you down.

In the tunnel, we see the flickering lights from the approaching train becoming brighter and brighter as the sound of the rattling tracks grows louder and louder. At this time, the music also becomes more frantic and the scene between SYLVIA and BARRIE begins to flicker more violently.

With adulthood comes sorrow and loss. There comes a melancholy awareness which never existed before. And how can you truly enjoy those things that you speak of, children and marriage and a career, when you know that the end is always lurking ahead?

SYLVIA You speak of death, Mr. Barrie?

BARRIE Yes, I suppose I do.

With this, the footage cuts out altogether. Suddenly the sound of the train becomes almost deafening. In the moment just before the train blasts through the tunnel, **PETER** *releases his grasp on the newspaper and leaps from the platform. The music and sounds cease abruptly as the light on* **PETER** *is extinguished.*

For a moment, everything is very still and quiet. Then, hundreds of newspaper headlines slowly begin to materialise all over the stage. They read such things as "Peter Pan's Death Leap," "Peter Pan Stood Alone to Die" and "The Boy Who Never Grew Up is Dead".

Then, through the darkness, we hear **SYLVIA**'s *haunting voice:*

SYLVIA But, Mr. Barrie, to die will be an awfully big adventure, don't you think?

Blackout

End of Play

ENDNOTES

Text

1 Barrie, J.M. 1937. *The Greenwood Hat*. London: P. Davies Limited.

2 From Barrie's person notebook [paraphrased]

3 Barrie, J.M. 1896. *Margaret Ogilvy*. London: Hodder and Stoughton.

4 Barrie, J.M. 1896. *Margaret Ogilvy*. London: Hodder and Stoughton.

5 Birkin, Andrew, 1979. *JM Barrie and the Lost Boys*. Great Britain: Constable and Company. Pg. 8.

6 Barrie, J.M. 1896. *Margaret Ogilvy*. London: Hodder and Stoughton.

7 Barrie, J.M. 1900. *Tommy and Grizel*. London: Cassel and Co. Ltd.

8 Barrie, J.M. 1911. *Peter and Wendy*. London: Hodder & Stoughton.

9 From Barrie's personal notebook.

10 From Barrie's personal notebook.

11 Barrie, J.M. 1911. *Peter and Wendy*. London: Hodder & Stoughton.

12 Barrie, J.M. 1928. *Peter Pan or The Boy Who Would Not Grow Up*. London: Hodder & Stoughton.

13 This and the following scene are a paraphrased version of a scene in Barrie's *The Little White Bird*. 1902. London: Hodder and Stoughton.

14 Barrie, J.M. *The Little White Bird*. 1902. London: Hodder and Stoughton.

15 Letter from Peter Davies to J.M. Barrie, written on July 2, 1916.

16 Letter from J.M. Barrie to George, written on February 14, 1915.

17 From Barrie's personal notebook.

18 Ansell, Mary. 1923. *Dogs and Men*, London: Duckworth. Pg. 26.

19 Letter from Dolly Ponsonby to Peter Davies, written on December 1946.

20 From Barrie's personal notebook [paraphrased].

21 From Barrie's personal notebook [paraphrased].

22 From Barrie's personal notebook [paraphrased].

23 From Barrie's personal notebook.

24 Ansell, Mary. 1923. *Dogs and Men*, London: Duckworth. Pg. 2 [paraphrased]

25 Letter from Mary Hodgson to Peter Davies, date unknown.

26 From Barrie's personal notebook [paraphrased].

27 Birkin, Andrew. 1979. *JM Barrie and the Lost Boys*. Great Britain: Constable and Company. Pg. 259.

28 Letter from Peter Davies to Mary Hodgson, written in 1934.

29 Barrie, J.M. 1928. *Peter Pan or The Boy Who Would Not Grow Up*. London: Hodder & Stoughton.

30 Letter from Peter Davies to Mary Hodgson, written on December 3, 1945.

31 Letter from Peter Davies to Mary Hodgson, written on April 28, 1954.

32 Letter from Peter Davies to Mary Hodgson, written on April 6, 1949.

33 Barrie, J.M. 1911. *Peter and Wendy*. London: Hodder & Stoughton.

34 From Peter's *Morgue*.

PROPERTY LIST

ACT ONE

Scene 1.1
Moving boxes
Books
Old photographs
Old letters
Bottle of gin
Packet of matches
Bottle of gin

Scene 1.2
Sweets
Linen napkin

Scene 1.3
Pair of britches
Sewing kit
Newspaper

Scene 1.5
Pram

Scene 1.7
Tea set
Bottle of medicine

Scene 1.8
Pen
Paper
Pipe
Pocket watch

ACT TWO

Scene 2.1
Suitcase
Dresses, etc. (to be put into the suitcase)

Scene 2.2
Bag of sweets

Scene 2.3
Handbag
Newspaper clipping

Scene 2.4
Pen
Paper
Piano (or some other such instrument, depending on the budget/ production)

ACT THREE

Scene 3.1
Books
Feather duster

Scene 3.2
Old photograph

Scene 3.3
Papers

Scene 3.4
Small notebook
Pen
Old photograph

Scene 3.5
Old photographs
Old letters
Newspaper
Telephone
Scene 3.6
Newspaper

ACT FOUR

Scene 4.1
Moving boxes
Books
Old photographs
Old letters
Briefcase
Papers
Newspaper
Tea set
Bottle of gin

Scene 4.4 (as with scene 1.1)
Moving boxes
Books
Old photographs
Old letters
Bottle of gin x2 (one full and one nearly empty)
Feather duster
Packet of matches

Scene 4.5
Newspaper clipping

LIGHTING AND SOUND EFFECTS

ACT ONE

Scene 1.1
Lights up: interior, evening
Sudden blackout

Scene 1.2
Lights up: interior, evening
Sound of laughter and clinking champagne glasses
Lights fade

Scene 1.3
Lights up: interior, day
Offstage crash
Lights fade

Scene 1.4
Lights up: exterior, day
Peter Pan statue projected onto the wall
Lights fade/transition

Scene 1.5
Lights up: exterior, day
Lights fade/transition

Scene 1.6
Lights up: exterior, day (as with scene 1.4)
Peter Pan statue projected onto the wall
Lights fade

Scene 1.7
Lights up: exterior, day
Offstage laughter and shouting
Offstage scream from Mary followed by cheers
Lights fade

Scene 1.8
Lights up: interior, morning
Glimmer from Barrie's watch projected onto the wall
Lights fade

ACT TWO

Scene 2.1
Lights up: interior, day
Lights fade

Scene 2.2
Lights up: interior, evening
Tick of the grandfather clock
Door opening/closing
Lights fade

Scene 2.3
Lights up: exterior, day
Peter Pan statue projected onto the wall
Lights fade

Scene 2.4
Lights up: interior, evening (split stage)
Music (either from a piano or what the production budget will allow)
Blackout

Scene 2.5
Lights up: interior, evening
Offstage shouting and commotion
Lights fade

ACT THREE

Scene 3.1
Lights up: interior, day
Door opening/closing
Loud bell
Lights fade

Scene 3.2
Lights up: exterior, day
Peter Pan statue projected onto the wall
Lights fade

Scene 3.3
Lights up: interior, early evening

Lights fade
Scene 3.4
Lights up: exterior, day
Peter Pan statue projected onto the wall
Lights fade

Scene 3.5
Lights up: interior, day
Telephone ring
Lights fade

Scene 3.6
Lights up: exterior, day
Lights fade

ACT FOUR

Scene 4.1
Lights up: interior, evening
Door opening
Offstage cry
Offstage sound of shattering glass
Blackout

Scene 4.2
Lights up: exterior, day
Peter Pan statue projected onto the wall
Lights transition

Scene 4.3
Lights transition: exterior, day (as with scene 2.3, though can be darker/ moodier now)
Peter Pan statue projected onto the wall
Lights fade

Scene 4.4
Lights up: interior, evening
Fireplace flames/shadows on the wall
Lights fade

Scene 4.5

Lights up: interior, evening

Projection of scene 1.2 (alternatively, this can be done using the actors onstage)

Sound recording of scene 1.2 (alternatively, this can be done using the actors onstage)

Music from scene 2.4

Sound of an oncoming train

Flickering train lights

Train doors opening and closing

Sound of train departing

Sound of another oncoming train

Flickering train lights – more violent this time

Blackout

Newspaper headlines projected onto the stage

THIS
IS
NOT
THE
END